MAKE
THE
MOST
OF YOUR
WORKDAY

MAKE
THE
MOST
OF YOUR
WORKDAY

Be More Productive, Engaged,
and Satisfied As You Conquer
the Chaos at Work

MARY A. CAMUTO

This edition first published in 2018 by Career Press,
an imprint of Red Wheel/Weiser, LLC
With offices at:
65 Parker Street, Suite 7
Newburyport, MA 01950
www.redwheelweiser.com
www.careerpress.com

ISBN: 978-1-63265-129-7
Library of Congress Cataloging-in-Publication Data
available upon request.

Cover design by Rob Johnson/toprotype
Interior by PerfectType, Nashville, Tennessee
Typeset in Palatino LT Std and Trade Gothic LT Std

Printed in Canada
MAR
10 9 8 7 6 5 4 3 2 1

DEDICATION

To Dad and Mom, who work so hard and with so much love for our family.

ACKNOWLEDGMENTS

I want to thank the people who have inspired and helped me to reach the finish line. First, special acknowledgment goes to my parents, brother, sisters, brothers-in-law, nieces, nephews, their spouses, and my great nephew. They each live and work with passionate interest in people, ideas, and our world, and they each create, explore, and contribute. They have cheered me on with enthusiasm and coaching throughout the good chaos of writing this book.

I am so grateful to Sharon Armstrong, an extremely generous and talented colleague; Marilyn Allen, my literary agent; and Lauren Manoy and Gina Schenck at Red Wheel, whose help was invaluable. Special thanks must go to Susan Devereaux, who brought her engagement, competence, and calm to our working relationship on this book.

Finally, thank you to Heather Purcell, Angie Arias, Frank Cole, Monsignor Sal Criscuola, and Gerald Anderson. Their positive attitudes about their work and their smiles always made my days better. Special acknowledgement and affection to Valerie Craddock, Carolyn Lomax, Laura Margiotta, and Kathy Ravenscroft with whom I have shared many great workdays and learned so much, including great dancing and singing karaoke at Foundations.

CONTENTS

INTRODUCTION

Get Your Hopes Up!

Consider that your workday has all kinds of wonderful potential:

- ✓ Income.
- ✓ Benefits.
- ✓ Achievement.
- ✓ Good relationships.
- ✓ Networking contacts.
- ✓ Fun.
- ✓ Status.
- ✓ A chance to make a difference.
- ✓ Creativity.
- ✓ Growth, learning, and development.
- ✓ A springboard to your goals and vision for your life.

Make the Most of Your Workday is based upon the belief that each workday is precious and filled with a blank slate of opportunities regardless of your workplace, role, and types of challenges you face. My goal for you in this book is to help you find insights, strategies, and tools to move toward being more productive, engaged, and satisfied at the end of each workday. For many people, that will involve conquering some chaos that can come from many places—including ourselves.

Whatever your workday demands and pressures (which vary among organizations, teams, and even individuals), there are some fundamental needs that we all bring to work. These needs led to the examples, strategies, core skills, and tools that make up this book, along with experts' research from science, medicine, health, psychology, business, and education. Yet, here is the hard part and the tough news: To fully put into practice any of these ideas, you may need to change. In fact, these strategies, skills, and tools may require a real shift in your thinking and assumptions and a close look at yourself along with your coworkers and organization.

This book is a personal challenge to actively manage and make the most of workday possibilities and problems. Take some control back, if needed, and do not wait for leaders, people, or circumstances to change.

However, we have to be real and honest about this harsh workday picture: feeling what it is like to see an email inbox that is always filled with new messages on top of older, unread messages (or opened messages that you closed because you couldn't deal with them); feeling what it is like to see long lines of impatient people at Starbucks, Home Depot, Whole Foods; knowing that the queue for calls waiting for customer service is off the charts; and seeing that the clinic waiting room has long run out of chairs and several people have called in sick. Most workdays include variations of these pressures along with emotional outbursts, exhaustion, and unreasonable expectations. Each of us has a finite amount of physical, emotional, and mental energy to manage all of these things.

Besides work, we have other people in our lives and things to do, such as:

- ✓ Family needs, wants, and responsibilities.
- ✓ Celebrations.
- ✓ Health-related appointments, activities, and downtime.
- ✓ Spiritual renewal.
- ✓ Education.
- ✓ Commuting.
- ✓ Community.
- ✓ Interests and enjoyment.

Then there can be more workday surprises—some totally unpredictable and others you might have seen coming: resignations, new minefields of changes to deadlines, emergencies (real and fake), and a general sense of uneasiness. People struggle to work together when they are not at their best, don't see things the same way, and have a wide range of personality and style. Technology can seem to be managing us instead of the other way around, and the dream of work/life balance is getting tougher and tougher to make a reality. Change and complexity of these changes is increasing while resources are diminishing. There is a frantic pace in many sectors, industries, and in both for-profit and nonprofit organizations. There are many people who struggle to just survive their workday much less make the most of it.

In place of resignation as a response to all the above, I want to stir you up so that you decide to not go home disheartened every day, but to fall back, regroup, reframe, and bounce back with new strategies. The book begins with four scenarios for readers to identify with and that are intended to inspire some "That's me, that's us" moments.

These scenarios are fictional composites developed from real workplace experiences, diverse industries, government, for-profit and nonprofit organizations, employee engagement comments, and from challenges shared in the author's workshops and training classes. The scenarios are intended to tap into typical workday challenges and to make an immediate emotional and intellectual connection with the reader. The scenarios are not based on specific individuals.

Do you identify with any of the following challenges?

✓ Getting caught up in the waves of office drama.
✓ Watching workloads increase with headcounts disappearing.
✓ Feeling your interest, enthusiasm, and focus at work fade.
✓ Yearning for effective leadership and more time.
✓ Wanting to avoid working with certain people.
✓ Feeling at the mercy of technology and behind with weeks of unread email messages.

These scenarios will show a link from our attitudes about priorities and coworkers to our communication and time management choices with needed skills such as adaptability, focus, and proactive planning for the unexpected. The scenario characters will have "Before" and "After" profiles throughout the book so that the reader can consider how proactive strategies and tools offer the possibilities for more productive, engaged, and satisfying workdays.

There are already many good and useful books, articles, seminars, talks, blogs, podcasts, and webcasts that provide strategies, tips, and tools to manage goals, priorities, time, and people. There is also growing knowledge with very applicable information from biology, neuroscience, psychology, health and wellness, education, and business and technology. *Make the Most of Your Workday* also contains strategies, tips, and tools—several of which you are already familiar with and may be using.

✓ Self-awareness.

✓ Identifying your needs and goals.

✓ Importance of mindset and self-talk.

✓ Priority, time, and energy management.

✓ Effective communication.

✓ Proactive planning to reduce or eliminate chaos.

✓ Reflection and action planning.

However, this is also a book about change because resources and knowledge alone *cannot* deliver a perfect workday, free of drama with coworkers or an ineffective leader or leadership team. In his book *The 7 Habits of Highly Successful People* Stephen Covey writes, "It becomes obvious that if we want to make relatively minor changes in our lives, we can perhaps focus on our attitudes and behaviors. But if we want to make significant quantum change, we need to work on our basic paradigms."[1] A willingness to consider changing some of our assumptions and ways of thinking, along with these strategies and tools can, however, empower and equip individuals to improve their workday experience. You are your own most powerful resource in this work.

Make the Most of Your Workday will give you:

✓ A straightforward approach to actively managing the workday.

✓ Practical strategies and tools that are linked together.

✓ Ideas to help you reflect on your current paradigms, mindsets, and approaches.

✓ Suggested actions and changes.

✓ Sources of information for additional knowledge and learning.

✓ Encouragement toward taking back some control.

My message is that we do not have to passively survive the workday, but we can actively manage and make the most of the opportunities that each workday presents. The workday gives us a good chunk of time to be and feel productive, engaged, and satisfied. The opposite can also happen and we can end each day deflated, frustrated, and disconnected. This book is focused on what individuals can do to make positive improvements to their workday. However, the return on investment grows powerfully when individuals, teams, and leaders partner with the common goal of increasing employee engagement, productivity, and satisfaction while conquering some chaos.

This book does not address the organizational side of the work partnership between individuals and their employers. There is so much written for organizations, leaders, and managers that is powerful and inspirational to build engagement, productivity, innovation, and to have a positive impact on the world. Organization leaders and managers have a serious responsibility and commitment to anyone they impact—their employees, customers, shareholders, constituents, and so on—and this book does not negate that role. Executives and other leaders may find things here that can help them both on the individual and organization level.

However, *Make the Most of Your Workday* is intended to encourage all individuals to choose action and leadership. Let's not wait any longer for the managers to leave, the next engagement survey, task force plan, or training class; let's take some control and make the most of our own workdays! With that being said, there are some ground rules for reading this book:

✓ Be open-minded and consider trying anything that you think will work for you.
✓ Share anything that you think will help others to have a better workday.

✓ Understand that there is no easy miracle, app, template, or hidden secret.
✓ You may have to leave your comfort zone.
✓ Take the time to reflect and question your own beliefs, choices, and quality of your current workday.
✓ Have some fun, rebel, and take back your workday.

I think that that we need to be engaged—whatever our role or current job—for our own happiness, productivity, and satisfaction.

Organizations need engaged employees (that's you too, leaders) for success. Employees benefit from an organization's success, existence, and growth. Organizations should create cultures that help engage and sustain that engagement for employees, *and* employees should do their part to bring their best self to work. It is a partnership that I see, not waiting for organizations and leaders to change. I am impatient with that waiting game and wrote this book as a call to action and assistance for all of us as leaders of our own workdays.

Today's Workday

Job Description:

- ⩘ Tough, very busy job, lots of distractions.
- ⩘ Expect constant change, chaos, and confusion.
- ⩘ Work with short-tempered, stressed, and over-whelmed people.

Job Requirements:

- ⩘ Bring high levels of energy, perserverance, strength, and resilience every day.
- ⩘ Be organized, flexible, focused, and capable of multitasking.
- ⩘ Maintain your enthusiasm, interest, patience, and dedication.

Today's workdays have plenty of chaos—and not the fun kind. Our different organizations have different varieties of challenge and messiness: From having 24/7 workflow when not really necessary to a lack of basic planning, coordination, and communication. Most people come to work to earn an income with the desire to be productive, engaged, and satisfied, and to go home feeling good about the day. However, that is easier said than done.

I want to tell you about the day before Thanksgiving last year. I met three strangers in Charlottesville, Virginia, where I went to visit family. I met three happy-looking, engaged, working people.

At a small kitchen china housewares specialty shop, it was a cashier's first day, as she explained; she was a retired nurse starting on a new adventure. At a beauty supply chain, a young woman told me this was her first retail job and that she hoped she would be ready for Black Friday; she was upbeat. And at a large grocery store chain, the cashier volunteered this was her first day on the job after staying home as a mom and how happy she was in spite of long lines.

Wow. Here were three people happy to have their workday. Thanksgiving cooking, tourists, and holiday shoppers: These are not easy jobs. Yet, they were engaged, productive, and more than satisfied; they were glad to be working. Being optimistic, I got the feeling they would sustain it or at least try to. It was easy to talk with them, and they looked energized when I became chatty too and wished them well.

It struck me that these three people looked like they were in the honeymoon phase of their work relationship. This thought led me to compare the work relationship to personal relationships with family and friends: We hope for a honeymoon phase that will help to sustain us when the reality sets in and we really get to know each other. Some days will be better than others, change and compromise are required, and maybe this relationship is not meant to last forever!

These three people will face threats to their engagement soon enough. I am basing my concern on some current workplace research that does not look hopeful and wondering about those of us who started out loving our jobs and those of us who are in jobs that we never wanted in the first place. Simon Sinek touches on this in his book *Why: How Great Leaders Inspire Everyone to Take Action.*

> Studies show that 80 percent of Americans do not have their dream job. If we knew how to build organizations that inspire, we could live in a world in which that statistic was the reverse—a world in which over 80 percent of people loved their jobs. People who love going to work are more productive and creative. They go home happier and have happier families. They treat their colleagues, clients, and customers better.[1]

Are you part of the 20 percent who have their dream job?

I included some generic job descriptions and requirements in each chapter since a lot is required to have good workdays and to stay engaged. An article entitled "Employees Are Responsible for Their Engagement Too" says, "Engaged employees begin the day with a sense of purpose and finish it with a sense of achievement."[2] Would you call yourself an engaged employee with a positive start and finish to each day?

Also, aren't our leaders, managers, and supervisors supposed to be there to help engage us? The article also points out that "though managers have the biggest impact on their team members' engagement, many managers are unwilling, unable or unprepared to motivate and engage their employees."[3] Are you one of the fortunate people with an effective leader and manager who creates a work culture that is engaging, satisfying, interesting, and oriented toward problem-solving?

The statistics that I just listed really worry me because in the Introduction I encouraged you to get your hopes up about workday opportunity. People spend a good chunk of time working, whether it is commuting to a workplace, traveling as part of our work, or working virtually from home. Each workday presents us with choices for how to spend our time, energy, ideas, and efforts, and brings us opportunities, difficulties, frustrations, inherited or self-created chaos, connections, or disconnections. Some of the choices we make will determine whether we leave work feeling good, bad, indifferent, or discontent enough to start looking for a new job. Once each workday is done, that chunk of time cannot be redone or recaptured as a "do over."

The next day will present more of the above and even more surprises and changes, and our mindset and resources will be tested again. That is the way it works. Additionally, if you are a leader who is reading this, you know that negativity can be spread just as easily as the positive spirit and results of teams making the most of their workdays.

Waiting for someone else to help us make the most of each workday is a passive approach that puts people in a dependent position. Those who work for and with a skilled leader and manager are very lucky, but a talented leader will not take the place of your own outlook, talents, and resilience. Besides, for many organizations, their own data indicates a serious need for effective leaders/managers and positive, accountable, and caring work cultures. I have worked for and with leaders who are effective, inspirational, unskilled, clueless, absent, and control freaks. I am sad to say that the effective and inspirational leaders stand out to me because I can count them on one hand.

Of course, there are many things at work that people cannot directly control. This book offers strategies and tools to help individuals make the most of their workday with the things that are in their Circle of Influence. Stephen Covey, in his book *The 7 Habits of Highly Effective People*, describes the Circle of Concern and Circle of Influence.

> The problems we face fall in one of three areas: direct control (problems involving our own behavior); indirect control (problems involving other people's behavior); or no control (problems we can do nothing about, such as our past or situational realities). The proactive approach puts the first step in the solution of all three kinds of problems within our present Circle of Influence.[4]

According to Covey, we have choices: "Whether a problem is direct, indirect, or no control, we have in our hands the first step to the solution. Changing our habits, changing our methods of influence, and changing the way we see our no control problems are all within our Circle of Influence."[5] We can get our hopes up because we have some key options:

✓ Survive the workday, wishing and hoping it gets better.
✓ Act to make some changes to improve the current workday.
✓ Move toward long-term goals and greater fulfillment, maybe that dream job.

Please note that even dream jobs have tough workdays as some of you who may be in your dream job already know.

The following is the first of several application tools throughout the book. This first one will help you develop your own "Before" profile.

Application Tool: Your Current Workday

Rate yourself on the following areas using a scale of 1 to 5 (with 5 being the highest and 1 being the lowest).

- ✓ How do you rate your own engagement at work?
- ✓ How do you rate your work satisfaction?
- ✓ How do you rate your productivity?
- ✓ How much unproductive chaos do you face at work every day?

Workday Challenges

Keep your current workday assessment in mind as you review several major categories of workday challenges. All of these situations can have a negative impact:

- ✓ Too much negative drama.
- ✓ Lack of focus and planning.
- ✓ Ignoring the need to replenish physical and mental energy.
- ✓ Lack of effective leadership.
- ✓ Overload of time, energy, and technology.
- ✓ Strained relationships or lack of positive relationships.
- ✓ The unexpected as the new normal.
- ✓ Keeping ourselves calm.

These situations are all interconnected with one leading to the others, as you will read in the four workday scenarios that follow. They are intended to capture typical challenges that many people face and are created from fictional composites from workplace experiences, employee engagement comments, and from participants in the author's workshops and training classes. The scenarios are intended to help you reflect on your own workday experiences and to start you thinking about something better. Do any of these examples remind you of your own workdays?

Scenario	Description
1	Drama, change, and the unexpected!
2	Please do not call us a team!
3	Where are the leaders?
4	What is so wrong with wanting to help people?

You will notice that the scenario challenges fall into one or more of these categories:

- ✓ Organization level: culture, change, strategy, structure, systems, and leadership.
- ✓ Department, group, and team level: interpersonal, collaboration, planning, and process.
- ✓ Individual level: self-management, interpersonal skills, and problem-solving skills.

The workday can be an active battleground with unproductive chaos and changes resulting in stress, confusion, and useless conflict. Let's start by talking about workplace drama. Drama is a natural part of working with other people in the midst of everyday work, changes, and emergencies. Sometimes drama is even fun or a welcome relief from boredom or stress. The main person in Scenario 1 allowed herself to remain in the drama longer than was good for her and her work. Even in literature, the story typically has an arc, a building up to a climax and then a webbing away and resolution. A natural resolution does not always come quickly or even at all, as you will read in Scenario 1. Sometimes, we have to create our own resolution.

Scenario 1: Drama, Change, and the Unexpected!

Nicole comes to work at a support department within a large organization ready to start the day. She is working steadily on a large-scale project with major deadlines looming. Her team finally has a leader they really like and have confidence in after a series of micromanagers and managers that were more involved in turf wars with peers than anything else. A text comes in from a coworker before she gets to the office telling her about the sudden and immediate promotion of her boss to another division. The manager is already gone, and the team is left in limbo and advised just to keep on with their current work. Before she sets down her things at her desk, another colleague pops his head in with "Have you heard?" Now, Nicole is not new to the workplace and has seen people come and go, but this one is like a sudden punch. She knows that the priorities for the day have not changed, but her focus is in danger. She has been to courses and knows she needs to make the most of her "best time," which is the morning. But this unexpected wave catches her and she goes with it.

Her own shock mixes with her pop-in colleagues' shock and then explodes into questions and conjecture. By the time her next-door office neighbor comes in, Nicole's emotions are kicking in, and shock turns to worry about what this all means for her and the project due in four weeks. The emotions of people vary from tears, anger, and of course, the ever powerful and understandable anxiety about what is going to happen next. Reactions vary from amateur detectives who use their networks to find out what happened to amateur therapists who act as sounding boards for others, and lastly, to amateur talk show hosts analyzing and expounding on their theories about the events. Then the rumors start to circulate about Lucy, the most tenured team member, making it known that she will apply for the manager job. Lucy's organization skills are valued, but her tendency to micromanage is a red flag. At least two department members make it known they may also apply for the manager job, and that leads to more emotions, including jealousy and fear.

On the organizational level, information is not readily available, but rumor has it that "they" want someone from the outside; on the individual level, there is the need to react, process, and vent about the loss of their manager before moving forward. Each day for two weeks, Nicole comes into her workday knowing that she has to get back on track, but there are more and more people coming in to talk, vent, and wonder. She too wants any information available, even the rumors and latest conjecture. Nicole is not interested in the manager job, but now feels pressure to protect herself and maybe go for it too.

She is not an unassertive person, but she is caught up on this wave and goes with the flow—or the undertow; she gets headaches that are not typical for her even on tough days. Nicole does most of her own venting to family and friends.

What about the project, you ask? Nicole did dash off an abrupt email to team members reminding them of their deadlines on her project. Nicole ignores her own milestones and goes home dissatisfied, depleted of her energy, and uneasy. She does miss her "real" work and the comfort and security that she had with her former manager.

Another major category for chaos at work is the lack of planning and collaboration, which leads to something similar to planting our feet in fresh cement. Silos often create overload, drama, and negative outcomes that spill over to a group of people, the ripple effect in action.

Scenario 2: Please Do Not Call Us a Team!

Take eight people in two different locations and expect teamwork and collaboration—I don't think so. Two members of this team, Jim and Carla, are opposites in communication and work styles, generation, needs, and experience, but need to work together without role clarity or authority. Their situation was bound to blow up for them and others around them. Jim has learned good workday survival skills from working with two different managers every six months: "Stay in your lane," give the loudest internal customers what they want and expect, and keep a tight boundary around your time and attention. Jim is extraverted, energetic, friendly, and well liked on the team. To be fair, the other team members pretty much operate the same way: If they feel like it and the task interests them, they will help each other. Being in separate work locations helps to support this solo mentality. Jim and Carla work from the same location so they cannot escape seeing each other.

Carla needs Jim's help on the large project she is leading, which was not staffed correctly in its initial project launch. Carla is frustrated and annoyed and feels like she is the only one asking for help with her project. Her style is intense and communication becomes aggressive when she thinks her project is in jeopardy and she feels threatened. She feels like she is tiptoeing around and meets various and understandable reactions to her requests for help:

✓ "Your project is not my number-one priority."
✓ "If you had spent more time organizing and had milestones, you wouldn't need help."
✓ "You were selected as the project lead, not me."
✓ "I might be able to help you next month."

Jim would actually like to help Carla but is hesitant to commit to taking on specific tasks; after all, these are not his priority. Besides, he has his own challenging internal customers. Jim doesn't feel good about not helping Carla and is actually interested in learning aspects of Carla's project that differ from his own; nevertheless, he continues to ignore her edgy requests for as long as he can. He knows that an explosive conflict with Carla is coming and would like to avoid that confrontation and explosion. He has seen Carla get aggressive with other people at meetings, and everyone ends up being uncomfortable. He nervously thinks it is better for him to stay in his lane.

They both go to the rest of the team and complain about each other. Sympathy abounds for Jim, who is seen as the innocent victim, while Carla is seen as the aggressor to Jim. Jim steps up his campaign and goes to their manager who advises him to work out things themselves since he is too busy to get involved with this nonsense.

The team members thought that finally having a manager would make things different and that the confusion, animosity, and errors would be reduced or eliminated. In the meantime, Carla grows more annoyed, overwhelmed, and disheartened; Jim and the other team members avoid her as much as possible.

Some of their work-related clashes were verbal and in public, especially when Carla found out that Jim went to the manager. She does the same and lists her complaints against him and demands action. A lot of time and energy is being spent on this; other team members and department people are listening, giving advice, and taking sides. Sadly, it is now personal between these two team members and spreading to others. Carla and Jim don't speak to each other anymore.

In this scenario, the people think that a leader will make a difference. As you read Scenario 3, you will see that the label "leader" does not necessarily bring focus, planning, and/or people development. Leaders are also caught up in their own workday challenges and have the additional responsibility of helping others be productive, engaged, and satisfied, sometimes in the midst of chaos. Everyone needs to manage their own priorities, time, and technology, and their own mindsets about their work.

Scenario 3: Where Are the Leaders?

Josh had his own big visions for his department, which is understaffed, but he plowed through on sheer will alone trying to move ahead with his priorities (innovation and new revenue ideas) along with volunteering every time his boss has a request. Josh has a team of twenty people who vary in generation, experience, personality, and career goals. Josh never challenges or questions new priorities from upper leadership, though he knows his team is stretched and working in a nearly 24/7 reality with the workday, including every evening and weekends; there is no line between nonwork and work. Josh decides to take a chance and assigns a large and complex project to Lucas, the most junior person on the team, who is highly ambitious but lacking the knowledge and experience for the assignment. However, Josh knew that the team member more suited to lead the project had made it known that she would not welcome the assignment and was at her breaking point. Josh was afraid this senior person might quit so he left her alone. Josh thought Lucas would jump at the chance to prove himself. Josh did not really want to hear his questions and concerns as Lucas got to know the scope and demands of the project. Josh tried to use compliments and his "I know you can do it" pep talks, which were not enough.

Flattery was what Josh thought Lucas needed: "You are the only one who can pull this off; the rest of the team will be envious. You will certainly be in the spotlight along with me when this work is completed and shared with the executives. I am giving you a great opportunity, and this is for your development!"

Deep down this leader knew that long hours and research could not substitute for real knowledge, experience, and expertise with this initiative and that the workload was uneven. He thought that if he could get more staff, he could spread out assignments more fairly. Also, he thought that these other members would aggressively object to helping each other. Josh knew Lucas was not the right choice, but he went ahead with the assignment and pep talks anyway.

Josh was already feeling like things were out of control; he never caught up on emails from months ago and tried all kinds of methods to get control of things. He abandoned the weekly meetings and happy hours the team used to like and instead ran around between management meetings trying to touch base with his team individually. He had good intentions of helping his team with ongoing development discussions, but discontinued these meetings for lack of time. Josh even tried a five-hour monthly meeting, but that exhausted everyone and didn't improve things. He didn't even have enough time to attend the new time-management webinar that was getting good reviews. He signed up for an online class, but ended up annoyed that the instructor expected attendees to refrain from multitasking and to participate. He thought that this facilitator had no idea of what it was like in the workplace; imagine, expecting managers to manage interruptions and problems and to be able to focus in the class. The lack of time and his incompetent team were his problems.

Was it time to look for another job?

Lucas, who had actively sought out the position in this group, started to realize that enthusiasm and drive alone would not be enough for quality results on this project. His work hours and frustrations increased and his family was growing unhappy. He finally had to admit that he didn't know how long he could or wanted to work like this even if it meant a quick promotion. It might be time to consider another path, team, or organization. He gave up trying to talk with Josh after Josh reacted as if he were complaining and being negative.

Josh also goes home late each evening and is exhausted and dissatisfied, wondering if it is time for him to look for another position. He came into this promotion with such high hopes and plans for innovation and revenue generation, but the organization did not give him enough of the right people.

In the next scenario, the relationship between manager and employee may at first appear to be positive and helpful. You may recognize yourself in the characters; there is even a higher senior manager who believes he is delegating when he is really dumping and is frustrated that people don't understand him. In this case, two leaders are creating some of the chaos for themselves while at the same time not developing their employees.

Scenario 4: What's Wrong With Wanting to Take Care of People?

Donna, a new enthusiastic manager, liked to be helpful and to take care of her team. She sincerely empathized with their tough roles in front-line customer service. Her team's workloads were heavy with mostly emotionally draining customer calls. Her caring side was a big part of her personality, and people gravitated to her with their problems, both work and nonwork related. For instance, Tom hated the new software and came to Donna with problems over and over again; Donna was very sensitive to Tom's dislike of the new technology. Team members knew that Donna would stop what she was working on to answer questions or chat, and they began following Tom's lead. The lines of people outside Donna's office were getting longer.

Donna's own focus and work suffered as she would stop what she was doing each time Tom or other team members appeared for help, encouragement, or just plain stress relief.

She ended up staying later at work and reluctantly taking work home, but would not turn anyone away. She usually went home feeling uneasy about the work she didn't get to do, irritated with herself and annoyed with Tom and the others for not learning the software by now; however, she was determined to not turn people away as their previous supervisor had done. Donna was determined not to be that kind of manager.

Donna's manager, Jeff, coached her about managing her time and delegating more to her team. Jeff was delegating more and more to Donna and knew both their workloads would increase rather than decrease over the next year. Jeff would surely get an award for calling it "delegating" while it felt more like dumping for those to whom he delegated. However, instead of following his advice, Donna is questioning whether or not management is for her and is considering stepping down as a manager.

Meeting the Challenges

We will take a practical approach to examining and improving the workday. This book is intended to help you to get the most from your workday regardless of the type of position or role you are committed to right now. Chapters are organized around the major challenges illustrated in the scenarios: change, people drama, leadership, work priorities, time and energy, communication, and managing the unexpected. The scenarios showcase these challenges in various types of roles and situations. Each chapter that follows will present a "Before" and "After" profile or makeover opportunity for the characters to use to improve their workdays. These stories are all linked together by multiple challenges and solutions, and all show a need and a critical opportunity for both formal and informal leadership in the workplace.

A workday needs a leader and that is *you*. To go home feeling satisfied, engaged, and productive, your approach needs to be proactive rather than constantly reactive or passive. Did you notice that several of the scenario people were passively waiting for something to change or for someone else to make things better? Don't wait for things to change or for someone else to do something with the things that are in your Circle of Influence. Some considerations within your Circle of Influence are:

✓ Self-awareness and self-talk.
✓ Personal and family goals.
✓ Attitude, mindset, and interests.
✓ The ability to prioritize, reprioritize, and negotiate.
✓ Planning time and energy around priorities.
✓ Effective communication and interpersonal skills.
✓ Response to change and the unexpected.

Here is your roadmap, a system of interrelated strategies, skills, and tools to help you manage and make the most of your workdays.

✓ Manage yourself.
✓ Focus on priorities.
✓ Value time and energy.
✓ Communicate effectively.
✓ Confront, challenge, and conquor chaos.
✓ Choosing change.

Summary

The roadmap will help to connect the dots between some common workday needs listed on the next page to the areas that are in our control, listed above. I have experienced for myself the workplaces and the workdays getting tougher over three decades and heard from hundreds of customers about their frustrations, anger, and unhappiness at work. This includes people working in local and federal government, nonprofit organizations, and diverse industries, differing also in size, cultures, and values. There are some common themes around what most people need (and what is often missing) to have good workdays:

- ✓ Wanting to have some control over their work and the workday.
- ✓ Needing clear and achievable work expectations.
- ✓ Having good professional relationships with the people with whom they work.
- ✓ Having some downtime to refocus, re-energize, and renew.
- ✓ Feeling connected and not being alone with problems.
- ✓ Being somewhere between boredom and unhealthy stress at work.
- ✓ Being treated fairly and contributing honest results to the organization.

You might look at this list of common needs and ask how we can fulfill these needs in today's workplace, especially the first one about control. And it is very true that there are many aspects of the workplaces and workday that we cannot control. In addition, outside of work we listen daily to and live through so many events beyond our control. We are in the midst of industry, organization, and culture change; competitive, technological, economic, and political challenges; efforts to employ, retain, develop, and engage people. So, it is critical to remember that we *do* have several important areas that we can control, and that is the focus of this book. As I mentioned earlier in the chapter, we can choose to:

1. Survive the workday, wishing and hoping it gets better.
2. Act to make some changes to improve the current workday.
3. Move toward long-term goals and greater fulfillment, maybe even that dream job.

We will focus on all three of these ideas. Sometimes surviving the workday is the best strategy, for example, "Let me just survive this shift." However, since constant survival mode takes a serious toll on people, the central focus of this book is on the second idea in the list. These same strategies and tools plus your own insights and realizations can also help you make peace with your current work situation and use your energy to make a plan for finding work and a role more aligned with your interests, needs, and happiness. Whatever you choose, it is important that you use each workday to be as happy as you can be, managing yourself through great challenges.

Let me share a very useful personal belief that has helped me to improve my workdays and to also change careers several times—the belief that it is up to me to go get what I wanted from all the jobs, roles, and career paths. I didn't think that anyone else was responsible for my ultimate satisfaction or happiness. I always believed there was something I could do even if that meant the difficult personal change, such as go back to school or train to learn a new skill, search for a new job, learn how to speak up, or stop working every Sunday to get a clean inbox when the nature of my billing job meant that that was never going to happen. (I wish I had learned that sooner and spent those Sundays having fun.) So let's roll up our sleeves and work our way through the roadmap.

Reflection and Action

Each chapter will end with a "Reflection and Action" section. To get the most from each chapter, reflect and assess your typical workday by answering the following questions and recording your responses in your best place for keeping notes (smart phone, notebook, tablet).

Take some time now and note the scenario and characters that resonate with you, reminding you of yourself, your coworkers, your boss, and/or your situations. Then reflect on the following questions and complete the actions.

Reflection

- ✓ What does it take for you to have a good workday?
- ✓ How often do you have these good workdays?
- ✓ How do you feel at the end of these good workdays?

Action

Make a list of your current challenges that prevent you from having a good workday most of the time. Keep your list to refer to as you read ahead.

Manage Yourself—It's All About You

Job Requirements (continued):

- ⌄ Must consistently manage mood.
- ⌄ Take responsibility for one's actions and work.
- ⌄ Stay confident and calm when things go wrong.
- ⌄ Appreciate opportunity.

Let's talk about why we are starting with Manage Yourself instead of managing priorities, time, or communication. Because it all starts with us; we own our workday and the responsibility for making the most of it. Since the central focus of this book is the belief that the workday is filled with opportunities for us, then managing ourselves must be the starting point. We are the main character in our workday regardless of where we are working—the street, an office, home, traveling, a store, or online. And it doesn't matter whether we are just starting out to build a career, temping and collecting a paycheck, getting ready to launch a new life phase, or somewhere in between.

We have to bring and maintain our best self at work to have good workdays. So this chapter is all about you. Let's use knowing ourselves and managing ourselves to build the foundation to help us work effectively in any organizational culture, with different leadership styles, or managing various forms of work chaos until we find something that is a better fit for us. You will then have a great advantage that you will bring to every situation.

There are three ways to help us get this advantage:

✓ Increase our self-awareness.
✓ Examine our mindsets.
✓ Examine our self-talk.

Let's look at a "Before" profile for Nicole in Scenario 1. Remember that Nicole got swept up in the drama that resulted from the unexpected change of her leader suddenly leaving. These events were certainly not under her control. However, there were some aspects of her workday that *were* under her control, and we will explore them in this chapter. Instead of going home with headaches and nagging worries about her work procrastination, perhaps Nicole could have gone home feeling differently if she changed some of her behaviors and managed herself.

"Before" Profile for Nicole

Manage Yourself

✓ Wanted to be there for coworkers.
✓ Liked work that required focus.

✓ Needed this stepping-stone job for experience and tuition benefits.

✓ Wasn't ready to start her own business.

✓ Went home and brooded about continued uncertainty at work.

✓ Mindset: I don't want to go to work anymore.

Focus on Priorities

✓ Understood and validated work priorities.

Value Time and Energy

✓ Gave away time to everyone and allowed constant interruptions.

✓ Sometimes encouraged interruptions.

Communicate Effectively

✓ Did not say no to people who wanted to talk about organization changes.

✓ Sent direct emails to coworkers clarifying their roles on her project.

✓ Listened to coworkers.

Confront, Challenge, and Conquer Chaos

✓ Could not have foreseen the sudden departures of key people in her work life.

✓ Sought information.

✓ Validated her priorities with the interim leader.

You can see from Nicole's profile that like most of us, she had strengths and areas of weakness; she had her own motivations around work, and she saw this position as a stepping stone to something else she really wanted: to work for herself in her own business.

Let's leave Nicole for now and consider how the ideas and tools in this chapter could have helped her in an "After" profile to improve her workday. To build the foundation of being able to manage ourselves (which Nicole needed to do), we start with self-awareness.

Self-awareness

Self-awareness has several puzzle pieces that fit together to give us knowledge and understanding about ourselves. What do you need to know about yourself to help get the most from your workdays?

✓ Your personality.
✓ Your needs, goals, and dreams.
✓ How you behave and interact at work.

Daniel Goleman's critical work in leadership and emotional intelligence connects self-awareness with emotional intelligence: "Self-awareness is the first component of emotional intelligence."[1] Self-awareness is that honest understanding of our strengths, weaknesses, motivations, and actions, and the starting point is personality.

Your Personality

Learning about our personality is a good starting point for becoming self-aware of our strengths, preferences, weaknesses, and impact on other people. Learning about personality can also help us understand why we usually react the way we do, how we act differently under stress, and be an eye-opening "aha moment" that everyone is not like us.

The Encyclopedia of Psychology online (*www.apa.org /topics/personality*) describes personality as individual differences in characteristic patterns of thinking, feeling, and behaving. The study of personality focuses on two broad areas: One is understanding individual differences in particular personality characteristics, such as sociability or irritability. The other is understanding how the various parts of a person come together as a whole.

One common method to learn more about your personality is to take an assessment such as the Myers-Briggs Type Indicator (MBTI). Along with Myers-Briggs, there is DISC profile, CliftonStrengths (created by Gallup and championed by Marcus Buckingham), and others. I suggest that you consider using a personality assessment if you have not already had that experience. If you have taken one, take it out, dust it off, and refresh yourself with your report.

There are other tools that can also be helpful, such as the Hogan Personality Inventory or IPIP-NEO Assessment of the "Big Five" personality dimensions. In an article for the *Harvard Business Review*, Ben Dattner wrote about the Hogan Personality Inventory and the NEO, stating that these "are likely to identify some hard-hitting development themes for almost anyone brave enough to take them, for example telling you that you are set in your ways, likely to anger easily, and take criticism too personally."[2]

Being brave and getting to know our personality and other personality types may include learning about what causes us stress and how we react under stress. This information should increase our self-awareness in terms of workday needs. According to Daniel Goldman, there is also a mind-body connection to be aware of: "The physiological state of your whole body can drastically affect how you respond in a given situation if you don't pay attention to it. (For example, a study in 2011 indicated that judges hand down stricter sentences when they're hungry.)"[3] So if you are not eating well as part of having a good workday, beware of talking and sending email if you have not had a healthy lunch!

What does it really mean to be self-aware and to bring my personality to the workday? My personality prefers some quiet for reflection as well as time for connection and energizing. I am attracted to the big picture; too many detailed tasks make me lose energy and feel tired more quickly than others who love the order and creativity of forms, charts, and numbers. When under stress, my communication might become too direct and abrupt. When you and I work together, I may not close down the design soon enough since I don't see that need for closure that you might. When I feel like I am being attacked by someone, I will not shrink away. And, I am someone who definitely needs lunch before responding.

Recently, I said goodbye to a workplace in which I spent a year and a half as a member of a team. I thought I was communicating information about my work, next steps, and history to the rest of the team, but realized that I was sounding defensive (because I felt on the spot) and had to stop and figure out what was really going on. My intention had been to make sure I was sharing everything with the people who would keep moving forward with the work we started together. My focus was on the tasks and not admitting my variety of emotions of pride in the work, the loss of the team, and saying goodbye.

I recommend something I call an *emotion watch*, which is taking the time, especially during stressful change at work, to reflect on what you are feeling and thinking and how that may be showing up at work. This doesn't have to take up much time and the results can have a positive impact on preventing misunderstandings, lousy communication, and damaged work relationships.

Start by identifying the things you say and do when you are under stress. For example, are there certain tough words, impatient phrases, or questions such as "What do you need now?" that indicate you are bothered by something and not at your best? Are there physical expressions such as tapping your foot or rolling your eyes that indicate certain emotions are rising and may need to be managed? I like to get a head start and will identify certain times, certain meetings, certain people, and certain situations in which I need to be very aware of my expressions, reactions, and interpretations.

The workdays may be filled with tasks, deadlines, and problems, but the need for understanding our emotions and behaviors has not gone away. Appreciating our unique personality is part of the self-awareness foundation to show us what we need to be productive, engaged, and satisfied at work even in the midst of chaos. There are two other components of the self-awareness foundation suggested in this book. The next section will present the importance of knowing our basic needs, goals, and dreams for the future.

Your Needs, Goals, and Dreams

Why do you work? One of the reasons that many of us work is that we need and want to generate income for supporting ourselves and our families. In Scenario 1, Nicole said that she basically enjoyed her actual work, but the drama and change around her challenged her enjoyment and productivity. However, she also needed to work, wanted build up to at least five years tenure, and wanted to finish her degree under the tuition assistance benefit.

In the Introduction, I suggested that work could be filled with opportunities and potential such as:

✓ Income.
✓ Benefits.
✓ Good relationships.
✓ Networking contacts.
✓ Fun.

✓ Status.
✓ A chance to make a difference.
✓ Achievement.
✓ Learning and development.
✓ A springboard to your goals and vision for your life.

In return, the agreement has largely been between you and your organization (even if you own your own business) that you will give time, talent, and energy, and will complete tasks and projects that are part of your job description, contract, or goals. In return, the organization will compensate you (pay, benefits, incentives) and provide resources, a fair and safe work environment, and opportunities. But the work world has become tougher for organizations and the people who work in them, and this means the agreement may not be as straightforward as it was in the past.

We know from our own experiences that the agreement is being challenged, especially as evidenced by employee engagement, retention, productivity, morale, and profits. Much attention and money is being spent to understand and improve engagement numbers while at the same time linking engagement to organization success. Various thought leaders, researchers, and organizations like Gallup have studied employee satisfaction, engagement, productivity, and loyalty; and the picture does not look good and has been trending downward. An article on *Gallup News* presents not only the low percentage of engaged employees but also the variance in engagement scores accounted for by managers. "Unless employees assume some measure of responsibility for their own engagement, the efforts of their organizations, leaders, managers and teams may have a limited effect on improving engagement."[4]

Therefore, since we have responsibility for our engagement, I propose that we not wait for the leaders and the experts to figure this out. We need to be part of determining what we need.

Going back to Stephen Covey's Circle of Influence, what part of this, if any, is under our influence and control? Understanding your own job satisfaction and motivation factors is a good place to start. Motivation changes throughout our lives; people can have more than one motivator at the same time and motivation varies from person to person. These are the various types of internal motivators discussed by Frederick Herzberg, Daniel Pink, and David McClelland: achievement, responsibility, growth and development, power, affiliation, contribution to mission, recognition, autonomy, mastery, and purpose.

I gravitate to Daniel Pink's three motivators of autonomy, mastery, and purpose[5] when I think of what motivates me today (and to different degrees in the past). I find these motivators help me to understand and manage myself at work. Even in my unhappiest of workdays during which autonomy or purpose was missing, there was usually something to learn and figure out about myself to improve either my knowledge or attitude. That insight and reframing are powerful tools that gave me better workdays, especially in those stopgap roles or jobs. This can make the difference between "I can't wait to get out of here" and "someday this experience will come in handy."

Mind Tools (*www.mindtools.com*) is also a good source for information to help understand motivation (and other topics). In articles and workshops, there may be discussion and disagreement on whether or not managers motivate their team members. However, the motivational factors included above are a natural part of individuals and, although effective managers create a work environment that allows team members to tap into their own internal motivation, individuals do not have to wait on someone else to figure out their drives, needs, and dreams in order to seek opportunities.

So what is your current situation and how does your role or job match up with your current motivation?

Application Tool: What Kind of Job Do You Have?

At this point, it will be good for you to stop and consider what type of a job you have or role you play in your current position and organization:

✓ I have my dream job right now.
✓ My current job is one more step toward the job/role I really want.
✓ My current job will lead me right to the job I have worked for and dreamed about.
✓ My current job is a stopgap measure while I earn an income and plan and set goals for the job/role I seek.
✓ Other (your description).

With all the harsh reality, data, analysis, and spotlight on disengagement and stress from workday challenges, it is important to take a balanced look at our needs, expectations met, and what we gain from work. The next tool can help us to gain this perspective.

Application Tool: Workday Balance Reflection

This is an important tool to guide your reflection on gaining a balanced perspective of your current work situation. In the middle of day-to-day survival, it is easy to forget, miss, and overlook some important factors:

✓ What drew you to your organization's mission in the first place.

✓ Your own development, growth, and progress.
✓ Your long-term goals, dreams, and vision.
✓ Your progress and achievements (big and small).
✓ Your team and organization's progress and achievements.
✓ Pride in yourself, team, and organization.

In workshops we talk about how important it is to step away from work so that you can get out of the weeds to take a larger view, reflect, and talk to others who may even be strangers. This tool can be used to help you remember, consider, take action, and reframe some negatives into positives.

Take some time and reflect on your workday by noting what you are both receiving and what you are contributing. The following questions should be considered:

Part 1: What are you receiving from your work and organization?

✓ Income.
✓ Benefits.
✓ Flexibility (work from home, hours, schedule, and so on).
✓ Enjoyable and fulfilling work.
✓ Development and growth.
✓ Role models, coaches, mentors, and contacts.
✓ Good relationships.
✓ Recognition.
✓ Responsibility.
✓ Chance to make a difference.
✓ Status/prestige.
✓ Challenges.
✓ New skills.
✓ Confidence.

Part 2: What are you contributing?

- ✓ Timely and quality completion of goals, projects, and tasks.
- ✓ Teamwork and collaboration.
- ✓ Innovation and creativity.
- ✓ Positive energy and interest.
- ✓ Flexibility and openness to change.

Part 3: Compare what you are receiving with what you contribute.

Be sure that to remind yourself of both sides: all that you are giving as well as what you are gaining from work, which is sometimes easy to forget. What are your insights from the balance sheet? Does this confirm your assessment of your current role or job with your current motivation?

- ✓ Dream job.
- ✓ Stepping stone.
- ✓ Springboard.
- ✓ Stopgap.

How is your current work/job helping you get closer to your goals and dreams?

Part 4: What are your workday opportunities and next steps within your influence?

It's not enough to know your personality, style, needs, goals, dreams, and vision. There are two other puzzle pieces to find out: How are you acting and behaving? How are you perceived at work?

Workday Interactions

People bring a lot of stuff to work—their personality, attitude, motivations, needs, and goals—and usually interact with many people (even if working in a virtual environment). Here is where the rubber meets the road: How do you and the other people you work with treat each other?

The good news about our interactions and behavior is that we can change our behavior. Many of us would like to change other people's behavior and, for the most part, we know that can be pretty tough to do. Come on now, it's hard enough to change our own. So our first focus is on ourselves and how we are perceived at work by others—in person, at a conference, on the phone, or in a text or email.

First let's go back and consider all that stuff that we bring with us to work. Visualize the tip of an iceberg of which we only see a small part of what lies beneath the water. Our tip of the iceberg is our behavior (visual, vocal, and verbal) that other people see and react to. Typically we don't necessarily see a person's values, beliefs, dreams, past experiences, emotions; these can be hidden below the surface. There can be a wide gap between our intentions (that people at work may not know) and our behavior, along with the interpretations that people make based on our behavior.

As human beings we are constantly taking in information, interpreting that information, and forming our perceptions. You can imagine how under normal circumstances there is a lot of room for misunderstanding each other, especially when we don't know each other very well. Behaviors vary based not only on personality but also generation, national culture, and gender. So our awareness of how we act during the workday is a critical skill not only for our success but also the quality of our work relationships. Let's look at some situations to which we bring our behavior.

- ✓ Meetings
  - Pay attention to where you choose to sit. Do you seek out the same people or sit with people you don't know?
  - Do people tend to overlook what you say or do they speak up and praise or add on to your contributions?
- ✓ One-on-one meetings
  - If you disagree with something, do you speak up assertively or keep quiet and think before speaking?
- ✓ Large events
  - Do you join in exercises, volunteer to lead small groups, or step out with your smart phone?
- ✓ Casual conversation and socializing
  - Are you comfortable making conversation with people you don't work with or do you avoid getting to know people in this setting?
- ✓ Problem or possible problem
  - Do you stay neutral, curb your impatience, or dial up to your aggressive self?

The following is an example of when my behavior—the tip of the iceberg—had the potential to negatively impact my workday. I needed the emotion watch and mindset check to get it together. (This might apply to you when waiting to use a copier, printer, or for someone to show up to repair your computer.)

Recently, my workday included a summer Saturday working on a writing project. I got up early to be the first one at a local printing/copying/mailing center to print some documents. I was the first one there. I was ready to pounce, but held my impatience in check, or so I thought. The store manager was about ten minutes late and told me she was a last-minute substitute. I smiled for a moment and stayed calm. I confess that I did rush in ready to politely push over any other real or imagined people who might try to cut ahead of me.

I quickly signed on to the computer station I needed and was all set to print. However, the printer was not ready; it was disabled and tension started to rise. Oh no, this is not a good start. What now? The manager told me to email my documents to her and she would print them for me. It sounded like a good plan, so I followed her instructions. Time was passing and she appeared confused, looking at long lists of documents. I stayed on my side of the counter knowing that moving to her side was aggressive and not allowed. My usually calm and easy-going attitude was being tested and I asked what was wrong. The manager didn't respond and finally printing started . . . and went on and on. My fake smile was gone and I ended up going behind the counter!

Things got worse before they got better, but I will stop here. As I walked home, I had one of those "aha moments" realizing how my mindset and behavior could have been positive instead of negative. I also wondered what the store manager was thinking about me. She couldn't know everything that was going on in my workday; she only got to experience my behavior in her store. This was not my regular workplace, but if it were, I would have made a bad impression on a coworker.

Let's look at that workday through the lens of my beliefs, attitude, mindset, self-talk, and behaviors:

- ✓ I won't have enough time today.
- ✓ Going to that print/copy/mail center is always a gamble in terms of service.
- ✓ I feel like I'm already behind the day.

✓ My body language: tense posture, unsmiling face, rolling eyes.

✓ My voice: terse, clipped, impatient.

✓ My words: to the point, limited to questions and needs.

I could have used the following self-check and some feedback about my interactions at that copy center. I not only impacted my workday but had the potential to impact the store manager for the better or worse.

Application Tool: Self-Check

You can ask yourself these questions to help see your impact on others:

✓ Do people want to work with you and seek you out for advice and feedback?

✓ Do people feel free to critique your work or approach you?

✓ Can you disagree without getting angry?

✓ Do you often gossip negatively about coworkers?

✓ Can people trust you?

✓ Do you manage your emotions most of the time or do you usually react either aggressively or passively, letting your feelings take over?

✓ Do you tolerate or enjoy different personalities, styles, and generations?

✓ Do you know how to respectfully set boundaries and stand up for yourself with people—even those in positional power?

✓ Are you aware of your tone of voice, body language, and choice of words when you are under stress, pressure, or conflict?

If you don't know how you act/behave and what your impact is on others, what can you do?

- ✓ Ask for feedback and really listen.
- ✓ Seek a coach, formal or informal mentor, or role model.
- ✓ Review any feedback that you received in the past.
- ✓ Observe how people act when they are around you.

Many see the strategy and tool of asking for feedback as a strength. However, there are still some real challenges in both giving and receiving feedback. In many cases we lack a positive intention and skill to both give and receive feedback.

Jay Jackman and Myra Strober wrote about people avoiding feedback and fearing criticism: "Most of us have to train ourselves to seek feedback and listen carefully when we hear it."[6]

Jackman and Strober also wrote of the positive results from overcoming the fear of feedback. "Those who learn to adapt to feedback can free themselves of old patterns . . . acknowledge negative emotions, constructively reframe fear and criticism, develop realistic goals, create support systems, and reward themselves."[7]

This section has explored much of what people bring to their workday: personality, needs, goals, dreams, and vision, and our behavior. In the next section, the two remaining pieces of the puzzle—mindset and self-talk—will be discussed.

Check your mindset because self-awareness is not enough!

Now that you know yourself, you need to examine your own workday mindsets and test for effectiveness. I did this in telling you about my behavior that followed from some negative mindsets at the copying center. Webster Dictionary defines *mindset* as an attitude, disposition, or mood, and an intention, inclination, habit. Our mindset then becomes an asset or liability at work.

There are three more working people that I want to tell you about because I can't forget them even after very brief encounters.

The first was a dynamic executive talking to a group of managers at a leadership conference. She began her talk by telling the managers that she chose her mood each day. That made an impression on most people sitting there who worked in various areas of a changing industry. Many of these people knew that their work futures and lives were changing forever and had their own beliefs about these changes. The executive's words were a powerful self-disclosure and a challenge to this group of leaders who had varying attitudes, moods, and lots of issues—their own and their teams'.

The next person was a young college graduate, in her first job after graduation as a real estate rental agent. This was probably not her dream job. However, she brought such gusto, persistence, and good nature that I ended up choosing the rental property that she represented. I had several young competing agents at different properties, but none like her. This particular rental market was a tough one, with so much competition and varied pricing. When I was ready to walk away due to price, she would not give up, insisted that I belonged in that apartment, and worked with her manager to come up with a solution. I knew she was a great asset to her company because her mindset placed her above the competition. When all the other competing agents moved on to the next prospect, she refused to stop working.

On a recent taxi ride, the driver told me about working at a big box store. Although that job was not his dream job, his approach to working there was a positive one, which differed from some coworkers who would not bring their best. He distinguished himself in his work ethic and also told me about his hidden skills: organizing, managing logistics, and leading others. He was concerned that he didn't have a degree. I hope he went on to get the degree but I think he was far ahead in managing himself and his mindset. I've seen enough to know that education alone will not guarantee workday happiness.

What do these three people—with very different positions and status, and in different generations—have in common? They each had a positive and powerful mindset about their current position/job and brought these approaches to their day. Carol Dweck, the author *Mindset: The New Psychology of Success* (Random House, 2016), contrasts what she described as fixed mindsets with growth mindsets in her work.

As we have acknowledged that there are a lot things not in our direct control, let's look at a partial list of what we do control:

- ✓ Mood and attitude.
- ✓ Behavior and reactions.
- ✓ Involvement, interest, and ideas.
- ✓ Treatment of coworkers.
- ✓ Personal boundaries.
- ✓ Our communication.

That's a powerful list to start with, and the importance of mindset is getting more and more attention. Here are some examples of positive mindsets:

- ✓ I can always improve.
- ✓ Mistakes correct me.
- ✓ There is no limit to what I can learn.
- ✓ Challenge is a springboard.
- ✓ My attitude and effort create my future.
- ✓ Successful people are helpful.
- ✓ I will never give up.[8]

Could any of these mindsets be yours?

- ✓ This too shall pass.
- ✓ I am marking time and can't wait until this is over.
- ✓ It was a good day, not perfect, but I did the best I could.
- ✓ Another lousy day ahead with too much to do.
- ✓ I could learn a lot from this failure.
- ✓ I can't do anything about these problems.
- ✓ I will escalate when necessary.

It is not my purpose here to hand out mindsets; only you can, and should, choose the right ones for you. However, I strongly recommend that you examine yours and perhaps develop some new ones to help you be more productive, engaged, satisfied, and happier at the end of the day. Choose or create a mindset that really matters to you for a week, month, or any period of time. Focus on that one periodically throughout the day. Put it on your smartphone, office wall, anywhere visual reminders would be helpful. You could even set an alarm during the day as long as that does not become a negative distraction. Make your mindset check a positive interruption!

Application Tool: Workday Chats and Check-ins

Armed with your best intentions and positive mindset, you will be tested even before you head to work. Chatting with ourselves can be a tool and necessity to stay on track in our efforts to make the most of the workday. The following examples are key mindset check-in and self-talk opportunities. Review them to catch your self-talk conversation and timing.

Commuting

I hate having to take Route 95 again.	or	This gives me time to listen to music.
Will Metro Safe Track ever end?	or	This effort is making us safer.
Staring at phone messages is bringing me down.	or	This video is making me laugh.
How will I survive this day?	or	I should have planned fewer things.

During breaks

What a disaster!	or	You are doing well on this crazy day!
I will hate that team meeting; it is a bunch of phony crap.	or	I need to jot down some phrases to keep me from losing my temper.
I can't focus on this today.	or	I'll get up and walk downstairs for a break.

Going home

Oh no, the trek begins again.	or	The trip home was so smooth today!
I have to bring stuff home again.	or	I will feel better if do some prep tonight.

I don't know what your conversations with yourself are, but I do know it's better for me if I think as positively as I can throughout the day. I admit I have to watch myself a lot in order to get back to the hopeful talk.

Let's get back to Nicole (Scenario 1) and look at some changes that she could make to improve her workdays. Nicole faced an unexpected loss of her manager that resulted in some drama, lots of talking, and a loss of focus on the actual work. These are all normal reactions and results from change, even though on paper it may seem like no big deal. These changes *can* be a big deal when there are so many unknowns and we want to hold on to any stability we have. Changes and choices that Nicole has are noted in *italics* and include changes that will be discussed in the chapters that follow. However, notice all the options under the "Manage Yourself" section that Nicole does have and note that these are under her control.

"After" Profile for Nicole

Manage Yourself

✓ Had a need for focus, but also being there for people.
✓ Need this stepping-stone job for experience and tuition benefit.
✓ Went home and brooded.
  ■ *Balance task focus with relationship focus.*
  ■ *Keep your own goals in mind.*
  ■ *Manage fear and jealousy and don't apply for a job you don't want.*
  ■ *Go home and talk with someone and/or don't think about work and/or go do something fun and energizing.*

New mindsets:

✓ I appreciate my work and benefits.
✓ Uncertainty is the norm right now, and I am determined not to go home disheartened every day.
✓ I am taking back my workday!

Focus on Priorities

✓ Understood and validated work priorities.
✓ Liked her work.
  ■ *Get back to some daily focused "zone" (managing interruptions, distractions, emotions) for project.*

Value Time and Energy

✓ Gave away time to everyone and allowed constant interruptions.
- *Limit time listening to others vent.*
- *Block off time for focus and other time for work relationships.*

Effective Communication

✓ Did not say no to people who wanted to talk about changes.
✓ Sent direct emails to coworkers clarifying their roles on her project.
- *Good idea, but make sure you also talk to people so they don't think you are heavy-handed.*
- *Let coworkers know you understand that your project is not the only one still going on.*

✓ Listened and was there for people.

Confront, Challenge, and Conquer Chaos

✓ Could not have foreseen sudden departures of key people in her work life.
✓ Sought information.
✓ Validated her priorities with interim leader.
- *Acknowledge and find an outlet for her feelings.*
- *Continue to validate priorities with leaders.*

Summary

It would be great if all organization leaders and managers created a work culture that engaged employees in being productive, satisfied, and eager to come back the next day. If you are the leader, manager, or supervisor of others, please note that creating such a culture or environment does not necessarily have to cost a lot of money. But the return for your efforts might be more productive, engaged, and satisfied teams and employees as well as less chaos at work. However, this book advocates that people become their own leader and start by managing themselves. Remember: You are your own greatest resource.

Reflection and Action

Reflection

Look back on your Chapter 1 "Reflection and Action" notes about good days.

What did you notice about the challenges that kept you from having more good days? Was anything related to your personality, behavior at work, mindset, and self-talk? Where do you see that you have some influence and control?

Action

- ✓ Take or review a personality assessment.
- ✓ Establish or review your long-term goals and dreams.
- ✓ Seek feedback to increase your self-awareness and emotional intelligence.
- ✓ Develop your own positive mindset.
- ✓ Have a good talk with yourself at the beginning, middle, and end of every day and say, "Well done!"

3

Focus on Priorities—Yours, Mine, and Ours

Job Requirements (continued):

⩪ Someone who understands that activity
may not equal results.

I use this phrase in many workshops: leadership, time management, performance management, and culture transformation. I rarely meet someone in class or in the workplace who says they are not busy enough; this also includes me. If you look around where you work, I think you will agree that with all the activity generated from meetings, incoming emails and messages, and new initiatives, you would expect that great things are happening. In some cases, they are—saving lives in health care, reacting to real emergencies of safety, ethics, restoring power after storms, fighting fires, as well as other less dramatic but important achievements by organizations. However, in many cases, some of the activity relates to false alarms; redundancy; lack of focus, planning, and organization; and poor results.

In this chapter, we are taking the next step toward an engaged, productive, satisfying workday. Please note that I did not write "perfect workday." I don't think that we need to have a perfect day in order to make the most of our typical workdays. But there will be more about the difference between good and perfect workdays later.

In Chapter 2, I encouraged you to discover or confirm some personal and professional priorities, such as goals, dreams, and needs. This may be hard to hear for some readers, but I have to be honest: Organizations are not usually developed around our needs or even professional goals. If you are fortunate enough to be part of an organization that did form around your needs and goals or that does match with yours, you will still need to keep your engagement fresh to sustain your work relationship. We all need some match or alignment in the work partnership. Remember the application tools in Chapter 2, the workday balance sheet and analysis of the type of job/role you are playing in your current organization. I hope your reflections led you to see some areas of this match between your organization's priorities and your own. You will probably have to take some time outside of your workday to see the stepping stones, springboards, and even opportunities from stopgap jobs or roles. This will take time, but it's important that you find a balanced view of your situation.

At work, as you try to focus on your organization's priorities (as well as your own personal ones), there is so much competition pulling and tugging on your time, energy, and resources. The path forward from this tug-of-war is to become an effective priority manager as the first step for managing time, energy, and work relationships. Several decades ago, I first remember hearing about time management in the work world and training courses that were offered for adults. In the 1990s and 2000s, priority management took center stage as people looked for help and answers with the increased volume and complexity of work, the new technologies, global competition, and reduced resources. In the 2000s, managing chaos and our own energy began to get my attention in courses and articles. Today, research continues to help us (neuroscience, biology, technology, mindfulness, psychology, health and wellness) with workday challenges.

These priorities are incoming all the time, do not remain static or stable, and do not even appear to be logical. In her article "Time Management Training Doesn't Work," Maura Thomas writes, "Knowledge workers are so overwhelmed by incoming information, they spend much of their time 'playing defense,' operating without a clear picture of their total responsibilities. . . . The pace is frantic, with a new interruption every few minutes, so it feels like there is no time to stop and organize it all."[1]

I experience and agree with this idea, but strongly argue that we must still find time to stop and organize around priorities. The tough solution continues to be the shift from time management to priority management; this chapter is focused on the importance of understanding and committing to priorities as part of managing ourselves and making the most of the workday.

As part of your work in Chapter 2, some of your priorities may have emerged: short-term needs, longer-term goals, and dreams. In this chapter, we will explore your organization, department, and team priorities, and try to link and align them with some of your own personal ones.

Let's get started by going back to Scenario 2 and develop a "Before" profile for Carla and Jim. These two people worked on a virtual team and were pretty much siloed in their work. Carla was feeling overwhelmed with her work and showed that frustration to Jim in her aggressive communication and reactions. Their negative energy was impacting the larger team.

"Before" Profile for Carla and Jim

Manage Yourself

- ✓ Carla's annoyance with Jim and the team is showing more and more, especially at meetings and in emails.
- ✓ Carla's communication style under stress is to speak without filtering.
- ✓ Jim prefers to avoid conflict, withdraw, and try to hide his frustration.
- ✓ Mindsets are negative. Carla: This team is a farce; I am in it alone. Jim: Carla is always the problem; why aren't the managers solving this?

Focus on Priorities

- ✓ Carla and Jim each focused on their own priorities.
- ✓ Collaboration is viewed as an option or "nice if we have time."

Value Time and Energy

- ✓ Different team members overloaded at various times.
- ✓ Relationships determine getting help or not.
- ✓ A lot of energy being spent on negative emotions.

Communicate Effectively

✓ Deteriorating with snide remarks or silence at
  meetings and a lot of side conversations and gossip.
✓ Frustration and anger building up, but not
  addressed.
✓ Complaining and whining about team and work.

Confront, Challenge, and Conquer Chaos

✓ There is no time for this.
✓ This is the way it has always been on this team.

There are some opportunities for Jim and Carla who may
be adequate *solo* priority managers but are not moving beyond
"mine" to consider "yours and ours." If your activity is to
equal results, you have to become or continue to be a priority
manager who takes a broad perspective. We will come back to
these two people at the end of the chapter.

Your Organization's Priorities

Priority managers begin at the beginning by considering the
organization's perspective as a way to frame their own focus
and to plan effectively. Organizations hire or contract with
people to fulfill their mission, reach a vision, and achieve strategic priorities. The reason any organization exists is to provide a service, make a difference, fill a gap, deliver a product,
make a profit, grow, govern, inspire—you get the idea.

Let's begin with a very simple clarification of some key
terms that are often used in and about organizations:

✓ **Mission:** The reason that an organization exists.
✓ **Vision:** Usually a short statement regarding what
  an organization seeks to be and to achieve.

✓ **Strategic Goals:** Broad primary outcomes along
with approach.

Partners In Leadership describes key results as: "those
most important objectives that are prioritized as strategically essential to the organization's success and
which must be achieved. They should be memorable,
measureable, and meaningful for everyone in the organization, so that every person can easily connect his or
her daily work to the Key Results."[2]

Whatever they are called—key results, strategic goals,
the top three—these are critical not only for organizational
success but also for people's productivity, engagement, and
satisfaction.

Mission, vision, and strategic goals lead to long- and short-
term objectives, projects, responsibilities, assignments, tasks,
and activities—the "work" that follows from planning. Our
own priorities during the workday should align with the organization's top goals, be easily understood, and be clear to everyone. However, in the work world today, the label "priority" is
given to many tasks, projects, and assignments to mean "this
is very important and I/we need you to do it now." The challenge today is that everything can be called a priority or top
priority. The danger with that approach is that if everything is
a top priority, then nothing is, and the purpose of establishing
priorities is negated.

Because activity does not necessarily lead to results, understanding alignment and prioritization is an essential skill for
formal and informal leaders. Here is an example of leader-led

planning around priorities done with Post-it notes on a blank wall.

Application Tool: Aligning Organization Goals With Team and Individual Goals

I know a manager who held a team meeting and used a blank wall for some basic strategic planning. At the top of the wall he posted the top four strategic goals of the organization on four large signs: safety, customer service, company stock return, and employee satisfaction metrics. Below that horizontally, he posted the department goals that were aligned with one or more organization goals. Note: Sticky notes are disliked by some but can still be useful for others.

He then asked the team to record every task, project, and assignment individually on separate Post-it notes (the ten team members each used different colored Post-its) and to scatter them on the wall. Team members were asked to group their Post-its under the related department and organization goal. The manager then asked a key question: Is there anything you are doing that is not aligned to department goals? A "yes" answer led to a discussion:

✓ Why is time and talent being given to this task, activity, or project (value or risk attached)?
✓ Does this work belong somewhere else?
✓ Could this be eliminated without risk?
✓ Are you the only one who can perform this task?
✓ What are your top priorities and why?

Although this planning activity was a good starting point (and I share this example frequently in training seminars), there is much more that is needed for today's challenges and that can build on this planning process. The ten people were pretty much working on their own things. Each thought they could use some help and that their things were more important than the other priorities, assignments, tasks, and projects.

Later in the chapter, we will use a collaborative approach to make prioritization even more effective, but this leader understood the need to plan and align team goals and individual work with organization goals. (I will talk about groups and individuals who don't have such a leader at a later point in this chapter.) But at least this team had a good basis for:

✓ Working as a group/team to "see" larger priorities.
✓ Face-to-face conversation, debate, and discussion.
✓ Commitment to being on the same page.
✓ Developing collaboration and teamwork.
✓ Individual and team prioritization.
✓ Time and energy management.
✓ Even planning for the unexpected.

Effective priority management requires all of the above!

Prioritization Approaches: Solo, Silo, or Team Collaboration

Once there is clarity on your organization's priorities, groups, and teams, individuals need to prioritize their work. The application tool helps to set the stage and align organization, team, and individual scope of work, but there is still an ongoing prioritization that needs to happen. Prioritization—ranking work in the order of importance—is a process and a skill.

It's important to consider the special connection between Chapters 3 and 4. We need to rank work activities, tasks, projects, responsibilities, and goals so that we can plan our time. Mind Tools summarizes the benefits of prioritization well: "With good prioritization (and careful management of reprioritized tasks) you can bring order to chaos, massively reduce stress, and move toward a successful conclusion. Without it, you'll flounder around, drowning in competing demands."[3] With good prioritization, we ensure that our activity does equal results!

There are several different types of management and planning tools, one of which is a priority matrix used to sort and make decisions about what to work on and the reasons why. You may be familiar with (or already using) some types. The matrix tool is intended to help you make decisions about your priorities by sorting these into quadrants with different criteria. You will then have a visual picture of your different projects, tasks, and assignments where everything does not look equal. A prioritization tool or process is necessary before planning or scheduling your time. One should flow from the other, especially since we know that there will be incoming priorities, emergencies, interruptions, and chaos.

There are different types of priority matrix tools, and are resources in this book that can help you to find the best type of matrix tool for you. I use the concept and create tools that work for my different situations. My customers have also done the same thing. Many of the matrix tools included consist of four boxes, or quadrants, exactly like the following example.

A simple way to think of priorities is to break them down into quadrants:

1. Top priority (based on organization goals and risk versus opportunity).

2. Top priority and urgent.
3. Less important priority.
4. Less important priorty, but urgent.

Priority management will lead us to time management, so it is important to note the following observations regarding the four quadrants:

✓ Most people are spending more than enough time in the "top priority and urgent" quadrant.
✓ Most people are also spending time on tasks from the two quadrants for "less important priorty" and "less important, but urgent."
✓ Most people are not spending enough time in the quadrant for "top priority and not urgent."

These are the elements that are truly proactive with long-term benefits: planning, developing self and others, organizing, innovating, expanding networks and relationships, and so on.

If you want to understand where some of the chaos is coming from, then imagine the implication of many people in your organization not spending time in that proactive category. How much of your workday time do you spend in each category? If you are satisfied with your answer, then great. However, if you are like many people today who are frustrated and worried about spending too much time or too little time on certain priorities, then use that frustration and anxiety as energy to change some things.

The matrix tool is an effective individual tool and even more powerful when shared and discussed with your leader. This important step is critical even if your team is missing a leader or manager. Remember that Nicole in our first scenario approached the interim leader to make sure her current large project was still important to the organization. However, even with great individual prioritization, there are challenges to workload balance from time, staffing resources, and personality clashes as demonstrated by Jim and Carla in Scenario 2. Our individual priorities do not exist in a vacuum but within the larger set of organization priorities, group priorities or department priorities, and each team member's priorities.

Application Tool: Paper Plate Activity

This activity can be done individually or within teams and departments. Each person doing this activity needs one paper plate and plenty of Post-it notes.

Write down every task, assignment, project, and goal for which you are responsible on a separate Post-it note. Just brainstorm and write; do not think or sort on importance, resources, urgency, time, and so on.

Place all the Post-its on the paper plates and ask for reactions. Most people will comment on needing a bigger plate, more time, more resources, and more energy, which are all valid reactions in today's workplace. We are working under the assumption that resources are not added, and that staying later and later at work is not the best way to be engaged, satisfied, or productive.

Using a basic matrix, individually prioritize the Post-it notes. You can also use a six-box matrix variation or the four-box model presented earlier in the chapter.

The following diagram is a matrix variation I use that can be used individually and also with teams:

1. Top priority and urgent	2. Top priority (no urgency showing yet)	3. Delegate (could be given to coworker, intern, temp)
4. Less important priority and urgent	5. Less important priority but must be done	6. Up for question and discussion (value, redundancy, nice but not necessary)

We then have another choice in organizations: What approach will we take? The most effective priority management comes from a team approach rather than a silo approach. Since we face budget, skill, and time shortages with increased workloads, a new approach is needed. However, the silo approach is still entrenched in many organizations even though we use the word "team" most of the time when referring to departments and groups. Self-interest is necessary and yet hard to break out of as a total work approach.

Patrick Lencioni states that the self-interest expressed is normal: "What is it about us that makes it so hard to stay focused on results? It's this thing called self-interest. Self-preservation. We have a strong and natural tendency to look out for ourselves before others, even where those others are part of our families and teams."[4]

Lencioni wrote for leaders, managers, and facilitators, however, his work is included in this book to help those who will need to lead informally and manage themselves and their teams. We can relate to and understand Lencioni's thoughts about the individual's priorities overshadowing those of the team. Scenario characters Jim, Carla, and Nicole understandably come from a perspective of self-interest. Lencioni talks about placing collective results ahead of their own needs to as a remedy to that idea.

> This is probably one of the top two things that separate good teams from bad ones. On strong teams, no one is happy until everyone is succeeding, because that's the only way to achieve the collective results of the group. Of course this implies that individual egos are less important than team achievements.[5]

Application Tool: Team Matrix

To take this activity to the next level of shared responsibility for collective results, develop one team matrix. If you are doing this with a group or team, combine sorted priorities into one matrix. This will take some time and effort to collectively decide, agree, and commit to the following:

- ✓ Where do individual priorities fit into the matrix?
- ✓ What can be eliminated (a "luxury," redundancy, no longer needed)?
- ✓ What can be delegated within the team and outside of the team?
- ✓ What priorities may be in jeopardy?
- ✓ What priorities can move from a higher status to a lower status or even a "holding" zone?
- ✓ What are possible incoming projects on the horizon?

The following diagram is how the outcome of this approach looks visually:

Top team priorities:	Other team priorities:
Collaboration/delegation top team priorities:	Collaboration/delegation other team priorities:
Team ideas: Innovate: Eliminate:	Possible incoming work/projects on the horizon: Note: Spending time on team surveillance of what is coming/could be coming is a powerful and proactive way to conquer some chaos.

A note about those people who are needed to fulfill reactive roles: Your work may center on health care responses, public safety, IT trouble-shooting, escalated customer service, and so on. The nature of your work and role could require immediate reaction and response. In some ways your priorities are straightforward because you are supposed to be reacting and spending your time in the most important/urgent quadrant. Some would argue that time management training is useless for these people. I still suggest that even in highly needed reactive roles at work, there is a need for planning, innovation, preparation, and "down time." In Chapter 4, we will use priority management to plan time and schedules and even though emergency work can't be scheduled, there may be opportunities to spend time in proactive work.

Key Points About Prioritization Tools

There are various uses for a priority matrix sorting such as:

- ✓ Breaking down a project by deadlines or complexity.
- ✓ Including prioritizing email and meetings.
- ✓ Reviewing regularly, asking who may need help or have some time, negotiating.

A matrix is a good individual starting point but needs feedback and validation. A team matrix is a start toward collaboration and chipping away our silos.

An important note about visual tools: Do not underestimate the power of low-tech tools such as whiteboards and wall charts used in conjunction with high-tech tools to draw pictures that help us to comprehend information faster and to see connections between concepts. The actual act of writing things down is helpful to our overloaded brains. We can gather others around these visuals and brainstorm for even more effective solutions. We don't need another email to read; a picture or image is an efficient and welcome relief.

If you consider both the volume of things that you have to read in your workday and knowledge about the ways that we take in and process information, then the usefulness of images, grahics, and visual tools makes sense. Haig Kouyoumdjian, PhD, details this idea in his article "Learning Through Visuals: Visual Imagery in the Classroom":

> Research indicates that visual cues help us to better retrieve and remember information. . . . Our brain is mainly an image processor. . . . The part of the brain used to process words is quite small in comparison to the part that processes visual images.[6]

Check Your Mindset: Solo vs. Team

Do you recognize or relate to any of these mindsets?

- ✓ I know my own priorities and these other things are not in my area of responsibility.
- ✓ I may do favors and help sometimes if I have time and feel like it.
- ✓ I own my priorities and have responsibility to validate, revalidate, alert, negotiate, and/or ask for help.
- ✓ We are all responsible for department/team collective results.
- ✓ Everyone for themselves.

A true team mindset is not easy, and you have to begin with understanding, committing, and focusing on your individual priorities. However, if you and your team go beyond and move to a broader perspective and then collaboration, you will achieve both collective and individual benefits such as:

- ✓ Better productivity and quality outcomes.
- ✓ Better relationships among team members through getting to know each other, work styles, and strengths.
- ✓ Opportunity to grow and earn trust.

You can go home more engaged, satisfied, productive, and happier because you are not alone. However, just when you think you have sorted out these priorities, there are incoming helicopters (I see a picture of constant information flying in, some important, redundant, annoying) bringing new requests, demands, inquiries, and problems. Some of these are real emergencies—top priorities based on risk and value—and some are someone's new idea or question. In addition, priorities change, grow, and compete. Leaders come and go, stuff happens, commitments aren't kept, and deadlines are missed.

Before jumping up to abandon priority management, I offer three strategies:

1. Stay calm.
2. Try the priority shuffle to identify solutions.
3. Remember you are not alone and don't have to suffer in silence; ask for help.

Application Tool: The Case for Calm and Composure

Let's start with the need to remain calm, which some people/personalities may find easier than others. There is a leadership competency of composure, and in their book *FYI*, authors Michael Lombardo and Robert Eichinger suggest counting to ten. Our thinking and judgement are not at their best during the emotional response. Create and practice delaying tactics. Go get a pencil out of your briefcase. Go get a cup of coffee. Ask a question and listen. Go up to the flip chart and write something. Take notes. See yourself in a setting you find calming. Go to the bathroom. You need about a minute to regain your composure after the emotional response is triggered. Don't do or say anything until that minute has passed."[7]

Thinking about a recent work crisis, I remember that I stood up and walked around the room after realizing that my work was in jeopardy and that I needed to come up with Plan B quickly. Though *FYI* is written for leader development, let's view this competency as a must for everyone.

Five years ago I was working on part of the implementation of an urgent and highly visible company-wide initiative. This is a story you probably know well: A big new initiative with no extra resources and varying responses, engagement, and interest from those we could ask to take on extra work. Another person was coleading our part of the implementation with me, and we took turns leading the calm for each other. When the strain got to one of us, the other person would double up on composure so the other could vent it out and then get it back together. I remember one of my pep talks to her when we were working through the holidays, and I told her this intensity would last a few months until the first phase ended. I saw us as calm "warriors," and she told me that she has kept that image with her as she moved on to even tougher projects. In turn, when I lost my composure at another point in the project, I remember her direct but kind feedback when my communication to our small group of team members was too aggressive, even for an aggressive timeline.

Never underestimate the need and skill of keeping yourself and others calm. Other people (both at work and outside of work) can be great assets to help us remain calm and focused on priorities when any kind of chaos happens. The best workdays include relationships with supportive, honest, and positive people who are also trying to be engaged, productive, and happy at work.

If you don't have a predisposition for staying calm, some practical tips can be found at *www.selfthrive.com.* Mindsets and self-talks can help if you are increasing or building this skill from scratch.

✓ I will handle this.
✓ There is other help.
✓ I am not alone in this.
✓ Let me get up, move, and breathe.
✓ I have managed tough challenges before.

Some people also have techniques or routines they use to help them regain composure and calm. Music, photographs, moving around, humor, and the outdoors are some things that might help.

Application Tool: The Priority Shuffle

As we disussed earlier, some of us are in roles that are meant to be reactive: firefighting, medical emergencies, fielding irate customer calls, restoring power, and ensuring safety. However, for many of us, we are not intended to be in totally reactive roles. One of my client groups wished for something like focus but with flexibility. By that they meant that their work required remaining focused on their roles and responsibilities without becoming inflexible silos with the rest of their department and organization. This concept of *focused flexibility* is needed when priorities change, new ones come along, or there is conflicting information that arises.

The following chart can help you understand the concept of focused flexibility. Here are the concepts to keep in mind as you go through each stage of the chart from left to right:

- ✓ Know your top priorities for the day/shift/week.
- ✓ Check for incoming priorities at a time you predetermine/schedule (if you are not in a highly reactive role). If you are in a highly reactive role, you will probably not have this choice.
- ✓ Shuffle/readjust priority focus if necessary and keep track of "shuffle/readjust impact."

Manage any emotions (anxiety, annoyance) and have the mindset that you are using focused flexibility and tracking impacts of shuffling trends. You track these trends and changes as a way to be proactive and not in a repeatedly reactive mode.

Day's Priorities	Day's Incoming Priorities	Revised Plan	Shuffle/ Readjust Impact
A B C	D E F	A B C D	B incomplete C incomplete D started E not started F not started

This is not easy to do, but I know from experience that these actions make the difference between going home feeling lousy and going home feeling like it was a good day (not a perfect day). Build in the expectation that your plan is flexible and not meant to be inflexible. This may mean changing your own expectations and mindset about planning:

✓ Why bother to plan anymore; give it up.
✓ My plan is a framework of top priorities for the day, not a structure set in stone.
✓ If your plan changes, that does not make the day a failure.

Key Points for Priority Shuffle

✓ Not every incoming email, call, or question marked "urgent" is a priority worthy of bumping another; it might be or it might not be.
✓ Decide how many times during the workday you need to check incoming emails, messages, and so on.
✓ Be calm, take time, stop, and compare the day's chosen top priorities against incoming priorities.
✓ Make new decisions about your focus, time, and energy.

✓ Keep track of shuffle impacts and patterns.
✓ Communicate your choices, any risks, and request validation of your revised priorities and suggest alternative options, such as delaying incoming or assistance. (This will take strategic communication skills and is also a way to cut down on chaos.)
✓ The solution does not always mean staying later (lower productivity, quality, work-life balance).
✓ A shuffled workday is not necessarily chaos, just different from your initial plan!

Application Tool: Escalate—You Are Not Alone

One of the best skills I ever learned was when and how to escalate with the intent of concern for the work, myself, team, and organization. An essential skill for better workdays is to know why and how to escalate. Escalation: positive, proactive problem-solving.

Why Do You Escalate?

✓ Because a current priority—time, cost, quality, communication, resources—is in jeopardy.
✓ Escalation is not fault-finding, punishing, getting even, or a method to cover your back.
✓ Escalation is a part of professional accountability to solve problems and do good work.

How Do You Escalate?

✓ Let others know you intend to escalate and that your intention is positive, coming from con-cern for the team, customer, organization, and problem-solving.

✓ Let others know to whom, when, and how you will
   escalate.
✓ Invite other people or teams involved to also escalate, if they choose.

It is a given for most of us that one of the biggest workday
challenges is conflicting, growing, and changing priorities.
The priority shuffle includes ongoing communication with
other people; the paper plates can only expand so far and putting in longer hours does not result in productivity, accuracy,
creativity, health, or job satisfaction.

I have seen some people drowning with real work while
others have free time in their silo world, picking and choosing
their level of efficiency and effort and not considering team
or coworker needs. Managers and leaders, you also struggle
with workday overload and yet many that I meet refuse to delegate for various reasons (Scenarios 3 and 4). It takes time and
thought, giving up control and knowing your team, among
other things. Some of you know the workloads are uneven
and lean on certain people, ignoring the capacity of others. If
you are not a manager, don't suffer in silence; speak up professionally and strategically, and learn how to escalate. Anger
and resentment won't help, however, I encourage you to go on
record with suggestions, collaborative ideas, requests for help,
and confirmation of priorities.

Let's return to Jim and Carla and do an "After" profile
for them. Remember how their verbal and public conflicts at
work were growing and negatively impacting the people they
worked with? They were engaged in work and personality
conflicts and wanted their manager to intervene, but they did
have some other options.

"After" Profile for Carla and Jim

Manage Yourself

- ✓ Carla's annoyance with Jim and the team is showing more and more, especially at meetings and in emails.
- ✓ Carla's communication style under stress is to speak out without filtering.
- ✓ Jim prefers to avoid conflict, withdraw, and try to hide his frustration.
- ✓ Mindsets are negative. Carla: This team is a farce; I am in it alone. Jim: Carla is always the problem; why aren't the managers solving this?
  - *Be open and see that other people on the team have needs and pressures.*
  - *Value relationships along with task completion.*
  - *New mindset: View yourself as a leader capable of collaborating and problem-solving with team members.*

Focus on Priorities

- ✓ Carla and Jim each focused on their own priorities.
- ✓ Collaboration is viewed as an option or "nice if we have time."
  - *Don't wait for a leader; lead yourselves.*
  - *Use the wide lens/a team matrix to go beyond your own individual priorities.*
  - *Delegate to each other as team members.*
  - *Specify delegation responsibility, authority, and deliverables.*
  - *Treat delegation with the same serious commitment to quality delivery that you bring to your primary priorities.*

■ *Be proactive if you meet challenges, including from other assignments; do not just ditch your team member's work.*

Value Time and Energy

✓ Different team members overloaded at various times.

✓ Relationships determine getting help or not.

✓ A lot of energy being spent on negative emotions.

■ *Be honest about your real use of your work time and availability to help others.*

■ *Be committed to giving your best attention and energy to completing tasks for team members.*

Communicate Effectively

✓ Deteriorating with snide remarks at meetings or silence, lot of side conversations.

✓ Frustration and anger building up but not addressed.

✓ Complaining and whining about team and work.

■ *Jim: Speak up assertively for yourself and don't allow sarcasm and nastiness.*

■ *Carla: Manage/stop your anger and aggressive communication.*

■ *Escalate for help if you have to; be positive and problem-solving in approach.*

Confront, Challenge, and Conquer Chaos

✓ There is no time for this.

■ *Anticipate project needs and think about what could go wrong (for example, people get sick).*

■ *What would be the contingency plan?*

■ *Who else could help?*

Summary

Managing priorities is a key necessity and skill in today's workplaces and is best done with the understanding that "mine" are not the only priorities. Collaboration with others is now critical for everyone's success and satisfaction.

There is a huge opportunity and need for leadership and management in many of today's workplaces. Since it is your workday, consider that even if you lack the formal title you can still lead and manage yourself and others to focus on results, managing priorities, and collaborative relationships. The book *Measuring the Success of Employee Engagement* points out that "leadership is not just for those who are in leadership positions. Leadership is everywhere. Every person can exhibit leadership by influencing others and by serving as a role model of what should be done or the processes that should be completed."[8]

Reflection and Action

Reflection

    ✓ Are you clear on your organization's priorities?
    ✓ Are you clear on your team's priorities?
    ✓ Are you clear on your work priorities?

Action

    ✓ Seek feedback to validate your self-assessment of your ability to remain calm and composed under pressure.
    ✓ Sort your work priorities using a priority matrix or tool that works best for you.
    ✓ Share with your leader and your team, and start the conversation about silos versus teams.

Value Time and Energy

Job Requirements (continued):

- ⌃ Willing to focus.
- ⌃ Willing to adapt and change schedule.
- ⌃ Willing to be a calm warrior.

As I began work on this chapter, I thought about my relationship with and beliefs about time and now ask you to think about your own. Are you and time friends, adversaries, partners, wary of each other, respectful neutral parties, or something else? Do you believe that time is scarce, limited, abundant, can always be found, or have some other belief? Your beliefs may impact your engagement, productivity, and workday satisfaction. Let's begin this chapter and part of the roadmap by acknowledging the need to understand and value time to make the most of our workdays. This will also include valuing and allotting some of our time to reenergize our minds, bodies, and spirits.

In Matthew Kelly's book *Resisting Happiness,* he states, "When we say we are too busy to reflect on how we are living our lives, it is almost certain that we are not busy doing the right things."[1]

Since I am currently at work on a deadline-driven project as I write this, this is a tough chapter to write. My own current relationship with time swings from thinking I have plenty of time to feeling like time is running out fast. I can think of ominous images that go along with the latter: big clocks with mean faces and that hourglass from *The Wizard of Oz* that the witch used to threaten Dorothy. I have taken time for granted in my personal life and fought against it. At times I find myself worrying about time passing before I finish the work instead of actually thinking about the work in front of me! I learned that this could very well be my way of distracting myself from the task at hand by going down the worry path instead of working.

In the last year, I notice some changes in my use of time. I have given more time to people at work and feel good about that even if some tasks get pushed away until later. I have become more aware of the connection between stepping away from work to come back more refreshed. I set aside large chunks of time for a project not realizing that the quality of work also required frequent breaks for mental, physical, and emotional recharging. So I think that like others, I have made some good uses of my time and then some not-so-good choices. So this is a "live" chapter as I share with you my own challenges and solutions. My hope for you not only in this chapter but throughout the book is that you find some things that work for you including insights, suggestions, or new inventions of your own.

It is exciting (and also intimidating) that in the area of time management there are so many experts, tools, books, articles, blogs, techniques, and good resources from a broad list of subject matter experts from: business, education, neuroscience, medicine, psychology, health, wellness, technology, and so on. There are also people who say that time management is useless. I had to ask myself what I could add to the current resources already out there; I too have tried different methods, struggled, experimented with tools, observed, and listened to people at work. I encouraged people to adapt a tool or to invent one that works for them. I realized that I can share my own insights, approaches, and tools that I've developed for myself as additions to the ongoing quest for tools and suggestions to help us manage time.

These insights, approaches, and tools must include thinking about our physical, mental, and emotional energy. I wonder if energy isn't the most powerful tool in our workday strategies. So this chapter contains both time and energy management strategies; we need to make good use of both. The good news about energy is that it can be restored and refreshed, unlike a period of time, which once used cannot be recovered. Also, we cannot manage time in isolation without understanding the links between priorities, energy, and communication. Notice "we" manage time; that is active not passive. Complete the following quiz to help you focus on your own beliefs about time. Answer true or false after each statement.

- ✓ There isn't enough time for everything.
- ✓ Time management is useless for today's workday.
- ✓ You can't plan for the unexpected.
- ✓ Planning is a waste of time.
- ✓ Meetings are a waste of time.
- ✓ Emails are taking up too much time.
- ✓ Interruptions are always bad.
- ✓ There's no time for friendly conversation.

✓ I don't have time for a real lunch.

✓ I need to complete or redo work that others could and should have done.

Your answers should provide some information about your current relationship with time. The quality of your workday is very much related to your beliefs and also your choices about time.

Like the people in the previous scenarios, we make choices about how to use our time and energy. Let's review a "Before" profile for Donna in Scenario 4. Donna was that new manager who never wanted to turn anyone away at work.

"Before" Profile for Donna

Manage Yourself

✓ Likes to take care of people.

✓ Caring.

✓ Empathetic.

✓ Wants to be a leader who is there for everyone.

✓ Irritated by people like Jeff, her manager, and his direct and no-nonsense style.

✓ Mindset: I should be able to do it all.

Focus on Priorities

✓ Reacts to people's needs and abandons her own needs/plan.

✓ No time to develop people so she could delegate.

✓ Not giving her top priorities her best focus.

Value Time and Energy

✓ Allows ongoing interruptions.

✓ Goes home overwhelmed and guilty.

✓ Quit company wellness walking program.

Communicate Effectively

- ✓ Doesn't ever say "No," "Not now," or "Let's talk later."
- ✓ Doesn't turn people away.
- ✓ Great listener.
- ✓ Says yes to her manager (that she will delegate more), but doesn't mean it.

Confront, Challenge, and Conquer Chaos

- ✓ Thinks she can keep going the way she is.
- ✓ Uneasy about growing chaos at home.

Donna has some important strengths in the area of caring about people and work relationships. However, those strengths alone were not making her workdays good or satisfying. Notice that "There isn't time for. . ." is often Donna's belief and response. We will come back and see what an "After" profile could look like, but first let's look at some things about time and explore the common outcry of not having enough or thinking we don't have enough.

Some Things About Time

Feel free to disagree, but I don't think there is enough time for everything and that includes the hundreds of daily emails, meetings, and requests that bombard you every day. I don't believe you can, or even should, do it all. I believe that we have to choose and that one of the major skills today is understanding, choosing, and committing to priorities at work and in your life. I am not saying that it is easy to choose, to say no at work, or to give up some things. However, I think we are already making choices but not necessarily feeling good about these choices. So here lies a major challenges and opportunity: Do not go home at the end of chaotic workdays feeling bad about what you did not do, should have done, or thinking that you "failed." It is essential to go home feeling that you did accomplish some work, that you did your best, and can make some changes tomorrow. Your neutral assessment of your tough days is essential to refuel positive emotions and help you get ready for the next workday.

In our workplaces and culture, the belief is strong that if we are competent and caring, we should be able to do it all and anything less is giving up. So in this impossible choice between doing it all and doing some of it, the results are grim:

1. If you do it all or try to do it all every day, you are probably overworked, overloaded, exhausted, and unhappy.
2. If you don't do it all, you are feeling guilty, incompetent, frustrated, and unhappy.

What about a third option to identify the most important things at work and outside of work, and do them well? That shift will not only require valuing time and energy but also a change in our beliefs and mindsets. Additionally, it will require organization support, which is difficult to address in workshops and seminars. I describe this as the shift from time management to priority management but within the framework of a positive mindset and not a default or defeat. Priority management is not just the alternative to survive today's workplace but it is the better strategy, regardless of resources and time constraints. Priority management was always essential even when we thought we had or really did not have more time during the workday. Maybe we had more time to waste?

Let's review some obvious key points about time:

✓ There is a definitive amount of time and money.
   For example, there are twenty-four hours in a day,
   just like there are 100 cents in a dollar.

✓ We decide how to spend our time as we do our money—with decisiveness, with consideration of results, or haphazardly. (Even if someone does schedule a mandatory meeting, I still need to decide if the meeting is a good use of my time and, if not, give feedback and other options.)

✓ When time is spent, just like money, it is gone, and we are left with positive or negative results.

✓ Not all time is created equal; you have better parts of the workday for certain things depending on your energy, emotions, distractions, and antici-pated challenges.

✓ Often we are not honest about how long things really take or acknowledge that we are not com-puters programmed to continue on endlessly with consistent speed and accuracy.

✓ We can make choices about our time that align with engagement, productivity, and satisfaction at the end of the day.

In my workshops I ask people to take out twenty dollars to pass forward to me. Everyone hesitates with annoyed or puz-zled looks on their faces; maybe a person starts to look like he is very slowly reaching for his wallet. I ask people to really tell me what they are thinking and finally people will call out "No way!" or "What do you want this for anyway?" I do it to make the point that most of us carefully decide how to best spend our money; however, if you think about your workday (which for many includes "after work" time), many of us find several points where we don't decide how to best spend our time, but just give it away to a random email, pop-in visitor, or ineffec-tive meeting. If we aren't willing to do it with our money, why should we do it with our time? Here are some good uses of our workday time based on the last bullet:

✓ Prioritizing work (Chapter 3): individual and team.
✓ Considering our personal priorities (Chapter 2): based on your development, learning, and relationships.
✓ Listening and learning from someone or just truly listening to someone.
✓ Attending only some meetings.
✓ Reading only some emails.
✓ Breaks to restore energy, such as music, walk, or a coffee run with a colleague.

Application Tool: Your Time Choices

On a scale of 1 to 5 (with 5 being the most satisfied, 1 being the least satisfied), answer question 1. Then think about question 2:

1. How well do you use your workday time?
2. If you had more time, how would you use it?

It's important to think about your answers, especially if you want more time. Learn from your answers to both questions and you could end up with more time. I think these questions can help to uncover some time; however, that will probably mean some behavior and communication changes for the individuals and teams. For me this is usually the toughest part of the solution!

Some Things About Energy

In the last section and in workshops, I asked if I could give you more time, what would you do with it. This is often a powerful activity and most people know right away what they would do with more time; the most common responses are usually "sleep more," "coach," "train," or "plan more." Most of us know immediately what is bothering us about time management: spending too much time on the wrong things and not spending enough time on other things. Often these "other" things that we wish we had time for are in the areas of family, personal interests, health and energy, better focus, communication, and collaboration at work.

In 2007 I read an article entitled "Manage Your Energy, Not Your Time," and it had a major impact on me. This article by Tony Schwartz and Catherine McCarthy categorizes energy as:

✓ Physical.
✓ Emotional.
✓ Mental.
✓ Meaning and purpose.[2]

Making the most of our typical stressful and chaotic workdays requires a lot of energy, especially to be:

✓ Physically energized, rested, and refreshed.
✓ Mentally sharp.
✓ Emotionally aware.

In his book *Two Awesome Hours* author Josh Davis adds, "The key to achieving fantastic levels of effectiveness is to work with our biology. We may all be capable of impressive feats of comprehension, motivation, emotional control, problem-solving, creativity, and decision-making when our biological systems are functioning optimally."[3]

Additionally, "Research findings from the fields of psychology and neuroscience are revealing a great deal about when and how we can set up periods of highly effective mental functioning."[4]

There has been good communication about the positive effect of exercise, movement, and nutrition on our energy and workday experiences. Our emotions also impact our energy. "Although we may not be aware of it, many of the tasks we perform—whether we're answering a colleague's email or engaging in a tough negotiation with a supplier—elicit emotions: excitement, anger, pride, boredom, uncertainty, anxiety, and so on."[5] This awareness is another important tool as we plan our priorities and schedule tasks, along with mental, physical, and "people" breaks (coworkers, family, and friends via texting, a phone call).

A Tale of Workday Warriors

I recently had an "aha moment" thinking about a workplace where I was part of a team that facilitated a four-day leadership training program. There was a lot of work, long hours, unknowns, things always went wrong, and yet I was working with four people who, in spite of very different personality styles and some disagreements, liked each other and loved the work. Our customers and company leaders appreciated us, so these workdays were great ones! We were exhausted physically, mentally, and emotionally on the last day. There were emotional goodbyes, feedback, and a major room breakdown and clean-up. We sat around unable to move. Those were great workdays, but not perfect, not easy, and not smooth.

I miss those four people; they all added to my workdays and life in ways I didn't realize in the moment. Besides time, I need some camaraderie and people to make the best use of all workday time. Without realizing it, our positive emotions about each other and the work energized us for the long stretch of mental and physical effort needed.

In contrast, I have also been part of many project teams where we did not achieve the same level of teamwork/relationships, customer engagement, or have the organization support to help sustain us in the tough workdays. Positive emotions truly do impact our energy and the quality of the time we spend at work.

We perform best when energized by positive emotions, but what do we do when the emotions are anger, fear, and anxiety? One way is to reframe and create some new stories as Schwartz and McCarthy point out: "Finally, people can cultivate positive emotions by learning to change the stories they tell themselves about the events in their lives. Often, people in conflict cast themselves in the role of victim, blaming others or external circumstances for their problems."[6]

In the previous situation, my colleagues and I called ourselves "warriors" instead of "survivors" as we got ready for those preparation and training days. That label, belief, and mindset went a long way when we had to deal with hotel Internet, heat and air conditioning failures, participant emergencies, speakers not showing up, food not delivered in time or at all, and by the way, other incoming work from emails and texts. You get the idea.

Connecting Time, Energy, and Focus

There is something else to factor in besides our energy when we manage time: Some work priorities require being scheduled at times of our peak focus and attention.

A top priority usually requires laser focus—your best time, your best self—for peak performance:

- ✓ Physical.
- ✓ Mental.
- ✓ Emotional.
- ✓ Necessary information.
- ✓ Willing and able to manage interruptions/ distractions.

Which of your top priorities (tasks, activities, and projects) call for your peak performance? Write them down to refer back to them later.

David Rock's book *Your Brain at Work* helps us go deeper into examining focus for peak performance. "[Researchers Robert Yerkes and John Dodson] found that performance was poor at low levels of stress, hit a sweet spot at reasonable levels of stress, and tapered off under high stress. The verb *stress* means 'to emphasize,' and it's not necessarily a negative thing."[7]

I relate this peak performance or "sweet spot" to the conversations in some training workshops when we talk about having to leave our "comfort zone" to enter the "change, learn, and growth" zone. At the same time, we also need to be aware of when we are spending too much time in the "unhealthy/unproductive" stress zone. We have often laughed and sighed in these workshops about having to leave our comfort to face that uncomfortable growth, learning, and change.

But my best experience and insights about focus come from leading live online training classes. The customers can be from any physical location, the producer works from his or her own location, and I am alone in my home office. The technology allows us to listen, talk, break into small groups, and chat without seeing each other. The computer screen reminds me of a stage.

Our Names	Center Stage Focus on a slide	Off Stage Producer chats
Group Chat	Activity Center Polls, chat pods, small break-out pods	Off Stage Slides in readiness

The visual idea of a theater stage comes not only from my live online experience sitting in front of a computer screen but from reading David Rock's metaphor about the prefrontal cortex part of our brain, "the biological seat of our conscious interactions with the world."[8] I now use a visual that I developed that is similar to the stage diagram for my daily work plan.

Here are some things that I have learned about peak focus from leading these sessions:

- ✓ External distractions have to be prevented (signs on the door, cell phone in another room, ringers turned off).
- ✓ Internal distractions that arise, like the desire to check email on my phone, have to be rejected and put off. I can check when we are on the break. It's true that just a person's name in an email can tap into emotions and curiosity, negative or positive.
- ✓ I can pick up a worry, some ego concern, or other emotion when the class is over.
- ✓ Beforehand, I plan ahead for my snacks and/or drinks for the break.
- ✓ Standing, walking around, and stretching on breaks is needed.
- ✓ My preferred best time is the morning, but these sessions are usually held in the afternoon. I have to be in my best focused state: alert and flexible. I have to get into this state at any time these classes are scheduled.
- ✓ Focus with related "allowed" multitasking.
- ✓ I want and need participation in chats and via an individual microphone (these are desired interruptions or distractions).
- ✓ Content must be covered in an exact timeframe, and deadlines are real.
- ✓ The producer and I sometimes need to communicate behind the scenes.

✓ Technology can sometimes go wrong.

✓ Sometimes people send private chats.

✓ I feel like an orchestra conductor moving through slides, concepts, discussion, and content while at the same time engaging, reading, and sometimes responding to chat questions, humor, and comments. When I move off the slide for a question or someone's observation and go off to improvise, I also need to move us back.

✓ I am utterly exhausted when this live online class is over!

The first couple of times I did this training, I was self-conscious, worried, and more scripted, not in my usual flow since I could not "see" the participants nor could they "see" me. I think it was by the third class that I forgot about my self-consciousness and the class flowed as easily as it does in most face-to-face classes. In that session and since then, I see the participants in the virtual room just as if they are there. I have learned to prepare myself as well as the technology; the first few times, I blocked off hours prior to the meeting to make sure I could "control" everything. Now, my mental preparation beforehand does not take as long. My virtual training mindset is ready: This number-one priority for the next four hours is sacred time, requiring my best self. Aside from a family emergency, there is no other priority that should enter this time or my mind. I prepare beforehand and tell people that I will be in a live online class and will get back to them after a certain time. Even unexpected technology problems have to be managed while keeping things going through calm and true teamwork with the producer.

I couldn't work like this all the time nor would I want to. The insight that I gained from this work is to know that when

I need this peak performance, I can bring this type of focus. In some ways, this intensity for a few hours is easier than the rest of the choppier workday demands. So a good lesson from this type of work, even for less-structured priorities, is that we can bring the focus for peak performance with effort and self-control when needed.

Putting It All Together

I was at a meeting and people started talking about the futility of time management for firefighters and some health care professionals. We started imagining a class for firefighting professionals who don't know when and where their first priority—putting out fires—will occur. Some of the health care professionals with whom I have worked talk about surviving their shift and how traditional time management is not a fit. I would like to introduce a process that may work even if you are in a highly reactive job.

Sort your priorities; make sure you know the urgent and top priorities and also the top priorities that don't look urgent. Try to decide what type of a day it looks like and choose the day "model" and corresponding approach to time management. Schedule time in chunks if helpful and adapt if necessary.

Here are some different time management strategies you can try categorized by and based on types of real work days.

1. Survive your shift/day

- ✓ Realize calm is contagious (Rorke Denver has a talk with this title on YouTube and TED Talks).
- ✓ Gather people together for quick updates, ideas, and morale. "We are doing great."
- ✓ Don't worry about proactive tasks on your list. Not today; stay focused.

✓ Watch for opportunities for breaks for yourself and the team.

✓ Really leave the shift/day. Don't relive it immediately; set an endpoint if that happens. (For example, when you get in the car to go home.)

✓ Go home tired but satisfied that you did your best.

✓ Reward yourself in some way—even nice words to yourself matter.

2. No time for work/meetings all day

✓ Make sure you eat; try to walk outside if you can; stand up between meetings.

✓ Realistically plan fill-in work between meetings if it is not too draining. Try to tackle some lower priorities that are quick hits.

✓ Consider whether or not you have time to focus on a small part of a larger project or task.

✓ Reward yourself at the end of the day.

Long term

✓ Question if each meeting is the *best* use of your time.

✓ Question the value and effectiveness of the meetings.

✓ Offer suggestions and ideas to improve meeting efficiency and effectiveness.

✓ Come up with options such as sending someone else, rotating people, using technology for updates, and some brainstorming.

3. I had a plan, but . . .

✓ Stop and assess the situation; evaluate the need *and* results if you abandon your plan.

✓ Shuffle priorities.
✓ Try flipping things around to create a new and visual mind map of the day.
✓ Keep track of how often and what causes these plan changes so that you can later be proactive and problem-solve.
✓ Reward yourself at the end of the day for your skill in adapting to change.

4. A smooth day

✓ Spend some time catching up with people.
✓ Spend some time on *proactive* priorities.
✓ Look for collaboration opportunities or new learning.
✓ Reward yourself and celebrate this day.

5. I bring the chaos

Understand and accept the nature of the role you are playing. (I once worked every Sunday to get a head start on Mondays until I realized Mondays would always be crazy; therefore, it would have been better to enjoy my Sundays!)

Look at your own work habits. For example, procrastination on certain things that you don't like doing; being a perfectionist when not required or not being a perfectionist when the highest quality is required; not following up on deadlines when others drop the ball. You may also get some ideas from Chapter 6.

✓ Let go and delegate.
✓ Ask for help.
✓ Reward yourself *and* consider making some changes.

Notice the differences in strategy for the different types of days, but also note these *consistent* time-management strategies:

- ✓ Go home feeling satisfied that you did your best.
- ✓ Be kind to yourself and others about less than perfect workdays.
- ✓ Learn from your own and other's mistakes.
- ✓ Remember that our energy, both physical and mental, needs to be refreshed.
- ✓ Spend time even on the toughest days taking a break, seeing a friendly face, or listening to a joke.

Why is it helpful to identify the type of day from this list? Anticipating realistically what we know about our workday/shift helps us tap into our physical, mental, and emotional energy.

Application Tool: Seeing Time in Chunks

When I plan my day and week I "see" and use blocks or chunks of time whenever possible instead of seeing time in specific units of minutes, hours, or days.

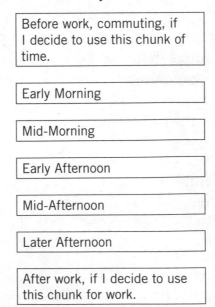

Before work, commuting, if I decide to use this chunk of time.

Early Morning

Mid-Morning

Early Afternoon

Mid-Afternoon

Later Afternoon

After work, if I decide to use this chunk for work.

I didn't include evening and nighttime because I wanted to show some limitation to the workday. You could include these other blocks of time either for more work or to include your family's plan.

In seminars, we have talked about chunking projects into smaller parts so that these parts seem manageable and not as intimidating to begin or to allocate time to. With time chunks (blocks of time), I see a more realistic tool for planning the workday schedule. We can get frustrated blocking the typical time slots of minutes and hours because 1) we may not realistically know the minutes or hours that we will actually have; 2) work usually takes longer than the time slot we schedule; and 3) I think using a unit of time larger than minutes or hours may be less taxing to think about.

Planning around time chunks give us more flexibility with realistic time estimates, a greater chance to feel "successful," and allows us to match not only time but energy needs. Interruptions and distractions will still have to be managed but there may be fewer of them if we are also factoring in our energy needs.

David Rock has good insight and background information on why chunking or breaking things down can work well. "The brain naturally wants to chunk anytime you hit the limits of what can be held on the stage. It's something you do without noticing."[9] The stage Rock is referring to is "the part of your brain central to thinking things through, instead of being on autopilot as you go about your life."[10] Just as grouping information is helpful for thinking, for me it's been helpful to think of time in these larger chunks rather than fifteen-, thirty-, or sixty-minute slots. The first step is to decide when your workday begins.

✓ Commuting: This is a time for reflection, planning, or nonwork-related activity like listening to a podcast or music.

✓ Designate a block of time for high-priority work, your best time.

✓ Factor in meeting blocks: Include time to mentally prepare for, travel to, and return from the meeting.

✓ Factor in blocks of time that include lunch, socializing, or even a short walk.

✓ Then decide when this workday is ending.

- Before you travel home.
- During your commute with reflection and planning.
- After dinner email or any other work.

People in highly reactive roles such as trouble-shooters, firefighters, and emergency workers often don't have time in a particular day to plan things other than whatever emergencies they are taking care of. Do these people ever need to meet to plan, organize, review, and/or improve things? Probably, but not on a daily or even shift basis. However, it might be possible to look at weekly or larger chunks of time and to carve out space for these proactive priorities and activities.

Even if you are not in a trouble-shooting role, but have found yourself reacting most of the time to the chaos around you, then it may be very tough for you to carve out proactive priority time on certain days. If that is the case, then visualize a week instead. Here's how an example of how this might look:

Monday	Usually more chaos and afternoon is taken up with meetings. Go with the flow.
Tuesday	Fewer meetings, and the morning time chunks could be kept for proactive high-priority work.
Wednesday	Regular task meetings take most of day and questions from the team are predictable. Don't schedule in a proactive priority like an innovation project.
Thursday	At least two time chunks could be held for high-priority work like that innovation project.
Friday	Usually more chaos with weekly deadlines looming. Don't overschedule; leave time for the possibility of work from a missed deadline by another group; use a chunk of time for reviewing and planning next week.

Some of my clients have one reactive/deadline-driven week every month. If that is the case, keep those weeks blocked out, fit in whatever you can during that time, do not plan major new activities for those weeks, and be as proactive as you can be in the remaining three weeks.

Just as thinking about the type of workday we face, thinking about time in chunks or blocks may help us to have wider perspective of time for proactive work and also for not thinking we have lost the day or the week or our best time.

Application Tool: Mind Map for a Day

The tools in Chapters 3 and 4 are meant to be visual images that increase their value both for individuals and teams. There are examples of making things visual on my website. The following list demonstrates the sections of my daily maps that I draw on paper, whiteboards, or online.

Categories for Mind Mapping

Top priority/focus chunks (proactive or reactive):

- ✓ Half-day team-building facilitation.
- ✓ New urgent proposal requested.

Energy chunks:

- ✓ Morning walk.
- ✓ Pack a good lunch.
- ✓ Social call to friendly person.
- ✓ Get enough sleep.

Other priority work chunks:

- ✓ New class design—draft one section.
- ✓ Review notes for team-building session.

Chunks for other tasks/activities:

- ✓ Check email.
- ✓ Make the fast and easy responses.
- ✓ Note the tougher emails for more thoughtful response.

Application Tool: Flipping Things Around

When the unexpected hits and you have evaluated and decided this new priority trumps your other work, try moving around your chunks of work from your mind map.

- ✓ Move the morning work to the afternoon to accommodate the new priority.
- ✓ Don't totally give up everything from the energy chunk.
- ✓ Move a chunk to another day, if need be.
- ✓ See if someone else can step in for you with some of the work.
- ✓ A change to your schedule does not have to mean that the day blows up or is ruined.

I was used to looking at the day's plan and believing that changes were always detrimental. I learned that if I stopped and flipped things around, I could salvage the day and stay positive. If your original plan revolves around knowing your top priorities, then you are making sure that your activity equals results!

Tips and Traps

Make Peace

Earlier in the book I wrote about working Sundays and how that was a poor time management technique. I was in a commercial billing customer service role and I wanted a clean start before each crazy whirlwind week. I didn't understand that the nature of the role was to react to the biggest problem and to just keep going. Working Sundays was counterproductive and unhealthy, and it made me crabby. Longer hours were not the answer. I had to make peace with the role because I had a history in that company and was not ready to leave. (I did end up leaving that job and applying for another job in the same organization.) Here are some other opportunities to make peace with:

- ✓ Make peace with selecting some emails and ignoring others.
- ✓ Make peace with not being perfect.
- ✓ Make peace with not attending every meeting.
- ✓ Make peace with choosing people and work relationships.

Counterproductive Focus

Be careful of a trap I fell into. I blocked off four months for one major project—a very important initiative for my career and a personal goal. That's fine; it was a lot of pressure but for a finite period of time. However, I didn't consider that this type of focus required both time and energy, not just four months of time. I didn't factor that in and stalled out halfway through, coming to a dead stop in the work. I realized my body, mind, and spirit were rebelling and that besides clearing the decks with major blocks of time for my big project, I needed to take into account too much sitting, worry, distractions of other important priorities, and getting some kind of a virus. I was also surprised to discover that I was lonely in the work and missed people. This makes me smile thinking of the times in workshops when people would laugh and say that most of the chaos comes from other people and that if they could be by themselves, all would be well.

My fortress of solitude wasn't working, and I needed to change up my plan. In my revised plan, the big project still got the biggest chunk of time for four months. However, I had to be more mindful about my other needs in order to get good results and have good workdays during the four months. I used a mind map to help visualize what the days should look like. I had to remind myself of other times when I was a warrior; therefore, I labeled this a "warrior required project" and marched on, but with better rest stops and short bursts of fun and work distraction.

Interruptions and Distractions

I have included interruptions and distractions as a source of some chaos. But I will preview a few things here for you to consider as you think about your time and energy:

- ✓ Some interruptions and distractions are necessary, welcome, and helpful.
- ✓ Sometimes, interruptions and distractions should be managed.

✓ Sometimes, we invite interruptions and
   distractions.
✓ Sometimes, we are the interrupter!

Donna fell into another common trap: deciding to do other people's work. Her reason had positive intent but also came with some negative results for her and her team. Donna was feeling overwhelmed by her priorities, her team's needs/interruptions, and her refusal to delegate.

"After" Profile for Donna

Manage Yourself

✓ Likes to take care of people.
✓ Caring.
✓ Empathetic.
✓ Wants to be a leader who is there for everyone.
✓ Irritated by people like Jeff, her manager, and his
   direct and no-nonsense style.

- *Reframe that being there for everyone all the time may not be the best development for the team besides putting you behind in your work*
- *Understand the benefits of being both empathetic and using direct communication like Jeff at times.*
- *Gain some insight about yourself. Why do you refuse to delegate and to speak up to your team?*
- *New mindset: I accept that my role has changed from individual contributor to manager and that this brings new responsibilities and skills to learn. This requires being open to changes in relationships and my own comfort level.*

Focus on Priorities

- ✓ Reacts to people's needs and abandons her own needs/plan.
- ✓ No time to develop people so she could delegate.
- ✓ Not giving her top priorities her best focus.
  - ■ *Identify her highest priorities versus doing people's tasks for them.*
  - ■ *Encourage the team to do the same.*
  - ■ *Set a priority of coaching her team to learn, be more independent, and to help each other.*

Value Time and Energy

- ✓ Allows ongoing interruptions.
- ✓ Going home overwhelmed and guilty.
- ✓ Quit company wellness walking program.
  - ■ *Set aside chunk of time to her focus daily or at least weekly and let the team know.*
  - ■ *Start taking your own walk outside periodically or commit to the wellness group.*
  - ■ *Set aside a good time for the team to ask nonurgent questions.*

Communicate Effectively

- ✓ Doesn't ever say "No," "Not now," or "Let's talk later," or turn people away.
- ✓ Great listener.
- ✓ Says yes to her manager (that she will delegate more), but doesn't mean it.
  - ■ *Learn to delegate work effectively and then do it.*
  - ■ *Set expectations about learning, trying to find answers, and the team helping each other.*
  - ■ *Ask people if and how they have tried to find the answer before they come to you.*

- *Learn to professionally push back on your manager when you disagree or have questions about delegation.*

Confront, Challenge, and Conquer Chaos

✓ Thinks she can keep going the way she is.
✓ Uneasy about growing chaos at home.
  - *Spend time getting team to cross-train and help each other.*
  - *Work and plan with your manager about work on the horizon.*
  - *Don't keep going the way you are; it will only get worse.*

Summary

I am happy to report that my relationship with time and energy has improved and that I have learned a lot about myself in the process. As a result, I have become more engaged, productive, and kinder to others and myself. My workdays are not easier or perfect, but are definitely happier.

Reflection and Action

Reflection

✓ Think about how you currently schedule your time. What challenges, if any, do you run into to?
✓ What are you doing to restore your mental and physical energy during the workday?

Action

✓ Choose a strategy, idea, or tool from this chapter that will help you.

✓ Start using this strategy, idea, or tool.
✓ Tell people what you are doing and ask for their
   support.

Communicate Effectively

Job Requirements (continued):

- ⌃ Knows one's own communication style under pressure and hot buttons.
- ⌃ Understands body language, voice cues, and power of words.
- ⌃ Stays cool and manages emotions.
- ⌃ Does not back away from conflict.
- ⌃ Realizes that everyone does not communicate in the same way.
- ⌃ Willing and able to adjust one's communication style to work well with other people.
- ⌃ Speaks up and escalates when things are wrong.
- ⌃ Knows when to be quiet, apologize, and listen.
- ⌃ Can say no professionally and wisely.
- ⌃ Uses influence and persuasion.

You cannot make the most of your workday if you don't communicate effectively. It's not just that the job requirement list for this chapter is very long. Consider what happened with my communication within less than six minutes when I felt stressed, overwhelmed, and behind in my work: I had a meltdown:

- ✓ I sent two tense (with annoyed tone) emails.
- ✓ I sent an abrupt text to a friend helping me.
- ✓ I left an antagonistic voice mail.

If this isn't an advertisement for effective communication, I don't know what is! This was not only my workday but also the workday of the four people who received my messages. I certainly didn't feel good about my actions and later apologized and explained my poor communication.

In my seminars we talk about how, under the best circumstances, effective communication is so challenging between people who are sending, receiving, and deciphering messages. A simple message of a sentence or two sent can be interpreted in so many ways by the receiver. I demonstrate by saying positive words such as "It's nice to see you today," but with a low tone, no eye contact, or enthusiasm. The participants in the workshop laugh and respond that they don't believe the actual words that I spoke. However, one or two people might respond that maybe I am not feeling well or have something on my mind. We have so much to be aware of in both sending and in interpreting messages.

And the previous demonstration is face-to-face communication; imagine the possible misunderstandings as we try to interpret what the various senders of emails and texts really mean when all we have are words (and emoticons) on a screen. (And even with emoticons, I sometimes have to stop and figure out the intended meaning.) We can also struggle with voice communication when we don't even have the body language clues to help us figure out the "real" messages going back and forth during conference calls.

So imagine the challenge in today's workplaces where we are often battling to be productive, engaged, and satisfied in the midst of chaos. Even in the dream jobs and workdays, there are expected challenges, the unexpected situations, usually stressed people, conflicts, and work overloads. And even if you don't experience these things, there is a good chance that your managers, coworkers, customers, and family are.

Besides these communication challenges today, effective communication takes time and thought, and these are often priorities/activities that tend to get dropped on tough days. Thorough and useful explanations, real conversations, coaching, and successful delegation all require effective communication skills and time. From both individual contributors and also many managers and leaders I hear:

✓ I don't have time to spell this out for you.
✓ I don't have time to talk with you over lunch.
✓ I don't have time to delegate; it's faster to do it myself.
✓ You understand what I need and the urgency, right?

There is some good news in the quest for having some control over our workdays: We have a lot of control over our own responses, messages, and interpretations from all the texts, emails, voice mails, calls, meetings, and walk-in communication.

To summarize:

✓ Work conversations are getting more difficult as conflicts arise more frequently and people are more tired, overwhelmed, and not at their best.

✓ We all have a story that we need to tell and under-
lying communication needs.

✓ It is easy to forget that relationships are of real
value—laughing together, coaching, learning,
understanding—and are an important part of our
workday happiness.

In this chapter instead of focusing on one scenario, let's
look at all of them. Each has people who are not communicating effectively, and this in turn negatively impacts workday
quality and adds to the chaos.

In Scenario 1, Nicole doesn't set boundaries with her peers
and allows and even encourages them to come in to chat anytime they want. Her emails can be too direct and interpreted
as arrogant.

In Scenario 2, Jim and Carla don't collaborate or listen to
each other. Jim doesn't assert himself with Carla and Carla
is too aggressive and attacks instead, thinking she is a good
communicator because she "says it like it is."

In Scenario 3, Josh doesn't speak up, ask questions, or push
back professionally with suggestions to his boss; he doesn't
really listen to people. Lucas doesn't set boundaries by talking with Josh about project concerns and hours spent working
around the clock.

In Scenario 4, Donna doesn't say no to repeated interruptions from one of her employees and doesn't delegate to her
team. She says yes to her boss when she really means "I won't,
but will say yes anyway." Donna's manager doesn't know how
to delegate, which requires clear communication and also
active listening.

These characters and their teams all suffer the impacts
of their communication styles, patterns, and choices. If you
relate to any of the characters, stay tuned for some alternative
approaches. Even if you do not relate to the characters, you

may recognize your coworkers or managers and gain some insights and ideas about your own responses.

Regardless of your personality, style, generation, motivation, priorities, role, level, or title, effective communication can make or break you. I have seen people from the highest levels in organizations to individual subject matter experts and contributors all struggle to be understood and to understand other people. I have shared with you how under stress, I tossed out all the effective communication guidelines like "Don't press 'Send' when you are tired, upset, crabby, or hungry." If you asked me for the most important skill for today's workday, I would say it is being an effective communicator. The person (whatever the title or role) who masters effective communication has a great advantage both in and outside of the workplace.

Our Needs and Communication

It's important to understand how effective communication is aligned with meeting our needs at work. Most people come to work hoping to do good, interesting work and to have good relationships with coworkers, customers, and their leaders. This positive assumption is one I first heard about in a process improvement class in which the instructor talked about most people not waking up deciding to go to work to cause trouble. The point then, and now, is that often the work processes or lack thereof may be the cause of chaos at work. We also hope that we are compensated as agreed and treated fairly and respectfully. Some also hope for advancement; others may not. Our organizations expect that we will do honest work as assigned and will treat others in the organization with respect.

This may read like common sense or you may be shaking your head as you read this. To be productive, engaged, and satisfied, we are balancing getting work done while dealing with other people. Although this may look superficially simple, we know it is not. This is something I talk about in workshops for managers, but it applies to all of us; we manage our workday balancing the attention to tasks with attention to the people with whom we work to accomplish these tasks. There is no formula I can give you for this balancing act; it's not a clean fifty-fifty split each day. I can share from my own work life that there are some days that are completely task-driven; I've had stretches of work time that are almost 100 percent task-focused with minimal people interaction; however, sooner or later the imbalance catches up with me. I did something radical a few weeks ago: I went with a team member for coffee and we talked about nonwork stuff. I knew this was "right" even though it felt weird. I had been neglecting this kind of human connection and I was struck, over the delicious cold brew and sitting outside, that not only did my team member and I benefit but so would the team and future work. For that hour we were just two people talking and listening to each other about our families, and I knew it was a good workday and that I had been missing this personal connection through conversation.

In Chapter 1 some common needs were presented:

- ✓ Wanting to have some control over our work and the workday.
- ✓ Needing clear and achievable work expectations.
- ✓ Having good work relationships with coworkers and colleagues.
- ✓ Having some downtime to refocus, reenergize, and renew.
- ✓ Feeling connected and not being alone with our problems.
- ✓ Being somewhere between boredom and unhealthy stress at work.

✓ Being treated fairly and contributing honest results to our organization.

You can see how being a skilled communicator would be necessary to achieve these at work. Let me add four other needs to be discussed within the framework of effective communication:

✓ We each have a unique story—style, goals, motivation, and preferences—and we bring this story to work. There are times that we need to tell that story and to be heard.
✓ We have a need to do good work that includes understanding and focusing on priorities and minimizing chaos.
✓ We need to expect and solve problems either related to tasks, people, or both.
✓ We need to be willing to really listen to others since other people at work have their own stories to tell.

The tools in the next section are some basics to help build effective communication.

Application Tools: Know Yourself

Chapter 2 was the first strategy section because of its importance as a foundation. It included knowing that our communication style under pressure is critical to a good workday. There is growing time being spent at work resolving disagreements, misunderstandings, and people drama. And, let's be honest, sometimes we bring the drama!

When CPP Incorporated, publishers of the Myers-Briggs Assessment and the Thomas-Kilmann Conflict Mode Instrument, commissioned a study on workplace conflict, they found that in 2008, U.S. employees spent 2.8 hours per week dealing with conflict. This amounts to approximately *$359 billion in paid hours* (based on average hourly earnings of $17.95), or the equivalent of 385 million working days. For example, *25 percent of employees said that avoiding conflict led to sickness or absence from work.*[1]

How much time do you spend each day or week dealing with conflict? It would be good to figure out the approximate amount of time that you do spend in dealing with, talking about, and recovering from conflict that goes unmanaged at work. Unresolved and unmanaged conflict takes not only your time but also your energy and focus.

Here are some key things to know:

✓ Understand conflict is normal. Conflict that is managed effectively can lead to better outcomes; unmanaged conflict can destroy relationships and quality outcomes.
✓ Know your hot buttons/triggers and how you react to disagreements, bad news, and gossip.
✓ Know the impact of your reactions/behavior on others.
✓ Figure out what you need to do to communicate more effectively in times of stress, disagreement, and concern.

Personality tools and other self-assessment tools like the Thomas-Kilmann Conflict Mode Instrument provide information that can help you understand how you act under pressure and some alternate behaviors to choose as a strategy when dealing with conflict. When I shot off those two emails and text, I didn't stop to think about my communication; I was just feeling that I was behind *and* possibly losing trusted help. Instead of waiting before pressing the "Send" button, I just reacted and endangered some good work relationships.

Set Some Boundaries

A basic need for workday productivity, engagement, and satisfaction is to be respected. This need may require us to set boundaries for other people to ensure that we are treated in a civil way that does not demean, insult, or ridicule. That also means that we respect other people's boundaries to ensure that they are treated respectfully.

Some of this is very obvious, and organizations also establish values and beliefs for all to follow. However, as stress and overload grow at work and different work cultures clash—including generational, functional area, gender, and so on—it becomes important to think about setting your own individual boundaries. The workplace or workday chaos is not a free pass to abuse, insult, or ridicule anyone at work. Sometimes, we have to set our own ground rules and realize that other people also have their limits.

I used the word "boundary" as part of effective communication for our basic workday needs. An article by Dana A. Gionta, PhD, and Dan Guerra, PsyD, helps clarify this idea. "What is a boundary, you ask, and why are they important? In essence, a boundary is a limit defining you in relationship to someone or to something. Boundaries can be physical and tangible or emotional and intangible."[2]

For the most part we are talking about emotional boundaries, though sometimes there might be a need to establish physical space between you and another person. But often what we see at work are people crossing boundaries of respectful communication by losing their tempers and speaking in ways that are insulting and demeaning.

How Do You Set Boundaries?

You need to be a skilled communicator to identify and set your work boundaries, which means:

- ✓ Being assertive.
- ✓ Understanding visual, vocal, and verbal communication.
- ✓ Listening to learn.
- ✓ Having courage and following up.

Here is a simple description of assertive communication: I speak up confidently, managing my emotions to solve problems with other people. I express what I need and listen to what other people need. Some examples of assertive communication include:

- ✓ "I need more help than you are giving right now; let's talk about the situation."
- ✓ "I need you to stop calling me names."
- ✓ "I need more detail about what you need/are asking for."
- ✓ "I need you to not talk behind my back and come to me with problems between us."
- ✓ "I need you to stop interrupting me at team meetings."

The boundary conversation is a good start but does require speaking up if things do not improve or change. We have been discussing individual boundaries, but teams and groups also establish boundaries with ground rules, norms, and guidelines. The challenging part is often following up to discuss adherence to these boundaries. This will take courage to address and the will to follow up. Boundaries will come up again in the strategic communication section: boundaries about work hours, responses to texts on weekends, and taking on new priorities. These situations require more than a boundary rather a professional and strategic problem-solving so that both parties get what they need.

Visual, Vocal, and Verbal Communication

When we communicate face-to-face, there are three components that help us interpret the emotional content of messages: visual, vocal, and verbal. The visual includes gestures, facial expressions, eye contact, and posture; the vocal includes voice tone, rate, and volume. The verbal includes the actual words we say. Effective assertive communication requires using not only assertive words and phrases but also assertive voice and visual components.

Assertive vocal guidelines: An even, moderate tone, rate and volume, with some inflection and expressiveness. Calm, firm, and direct.

Assertive visual guidelines: Confident posture, relaxed expressions, appropriate eye contact, and some gestures that add to the communication.

Assertive verbal guidelines: Words that are clear, specific, expressive, understanding, and helpful to solving problems.

I did not give you an inclusive list; this area of communication may be one that you want to pursue in more depth. I will share that in many of my classes and seminars this is the topic that many people identify as their number-one need. Did you realize that a smile gets a smile? "When I see your facial expression, I get the movement of your face, which drives the same motor response on my face, so a smile gets a smile," writes David Rock in *Your Brain at Work*.[3]

But it is also easy for us to misread each other not only visually but also verbally, especially if we don't know each other very well. I ask people if there is tone in email and usually there is an outcry of "You bet there is!" Think of words on a screen and the ways we either put tone into our message or read/interpret tone where none was intended.

The effective communication I mentioned earlier is not an exact science and requires us to remain neutral and assume positive intentions. That includes remaining open to understanding any generation, cultural, gender, or style differences that impact our interpretation of messages. For example, someone who crosses their arms may be chilly and not closing themselves off to your message or you. A younger coworker may not be unfriendly because they text instead of talking and an older coworker may not be lacking tech-savvy because they prefer to pick up the phone. There is no shortage of communication challenges.

Listening to Learn

Real listening is at risk during tough workdays. You know the reason often used by now: "I don't have enough time!" Let's define real listening as listening to learn, which means paying attention to emotions signaled by visual and vocal components along with hearing the words. And that will take time, focus, and energy.

Here are some other types of listening I have done and witnessed during the workday.

- ✓ I listen, ready to pounce when the speaker takes a breath.
- ✓ I jab in like a boxer ready to interrupt because I need to tell my story, my side of things.
- ✓ I called you back but didn't really want you to pick up.
- ✓ I listen and multitask (I think) and glance at my phone, glance away, stand up.

✓ I give you a listening look but am really thinking
about something else (the weekend, the next meeting, how not interested I am in what you are telling
me, that you said these things before and I don't
believe you).

You might recognize yourself or others in this list or even
have other types of listening to add to the list.

However, the rare real listening gets us to problem-solving,
improving things, reducing chaos, and repairing or building
work relationships. This deeper level of listening is not always
possible and necessary during the workday. Here are some
things that can help when it is needed.

✓ Identify situations when you really have to listen,
both in reactive and proactive situations and also
when the information is very important, complex,
or new.

✓ Know yourself and figure out what is going on
when you don't really listen before speaking. What
is on your mind? What is bothering you? What is
the source of your distraction?

✓ Tell the person you are distracted and schedule a
better time—focus, energy.

✓ Put aside temptation—your electronic device,
thoughts of your next meeting, vacation day, and
so on.

✓ Take notes; choose a listening body language. For
example, sit comfortably beside the person, not half
turning or glancing away.

If you need to really listen in a virtual meeting, do the
same as the above including making decisions about when to
not multitask with your phone and to put it out of sight. If you

have a one-on-one phone or virtual meeting, that is a time to bring your best listening and engagement.

Real listening is part of being engaged and engaging others at work. Some of you are members of or leading virtual teams over multiple locations and time zones. There are good tools about enhancing communication in virtual work environments. I know from experience that we have to work much harder to engage and communicate well in virtual situations. Some of you are having difficult conversations, coaching, problem-solving, and handling emergencies. Please don't forget to listen, which includes listening to emotions, questions, ideas, and problems you don't want to know about. Not knowing is a false, temporary haven and will only add more chaos down the road.

Challenging workdays require additional tools. You could consider the previous section as the basics and the next section as the advanced. I believe all of the basic tools and advanced tools are required.

Strategic Communication: Tools for Problem-solving

You might look at the following list and have a negative reaction to these words, especially "escalate" and "conflict." These are strong words, positive in intent, and mandatory to ensure good workdays! I link back to mindset and your possible need to reframe your experiences and beliefs about these action types of communication:

✓ Escalate.
✓ Collaborate/lead collaboration to manage conflict.
✓ Delegate.
✓ Influence/initiate/persuade.

Escalate

Maybe your think or have the experience in which escalation is a threatening work action. In the context of managing our workdays, I escalate because I care about the work outcomes and the work relationships and believe that there may be jeopardy to both. Escalation is not the blame game or "telling" on someone or covering for yourself. Here, escalation is a positive, professional, problem-solving action.

- ✓ I escalate—go for help, involve others—openly, assertively, and letting others know what I am doing and why.
- ✓ I escalate when I or we cannot solve the problem on our own.
- ✓ My language is professional, positive, and non-blaming but problem-solving.
- ✓ I escalate because I care about the mission, customers, team, public, and the organization.

For example: "We have tried to solve this deadline issue between us and it's not working. For the sake of the team, I am going to let Jennifer know that we need some assistance/ideas. I invite you to do the same with Frank."

Let's use Jim and Carla from Scenario 2 to figure out which of these approaches/choices is most effective.

- ✓ Jim goes to the manager alone to complain about Carla.
- ✓ Carla goes to the manager alone to complain about Jim.
- ✓ Jim and Carla go to the manager together for help.
- ✓ Jim lets Carla know he is frustrated and going to talk with their manager, and invites her to do the same.

What a difference an approach/choice makes to the relationships and problem-solving. There are situations when an individual should go talk alone with their manager. I am just suggesting that there may also be opportunities to work it out as a group.

Collaborate/Lead Collaboration to Manage Conflict

What if Carla and Jim in Scenario 2 had looked beyond their individual priorities, assignments, and success and really worked together? Imagine that all the conflict, sarcasm, bad feelings, and discomfort for themselves and their team could have been avoided. I am not saying that I think this is easy to do or that the manager should have taken a hands-off approach, just that they could have taken a different approach.

Effective leaders create a team culture that includes collaboration on all priorities important for the team's success. Effective leaders communicate team priorities along with individual assignments and expect specific collaboration, not some vague request for people to work together and support each other. But since I also know that effective leaders are sometimes in short supply, I question if you need a formal leader/manager to collaborate. I contend from experience that it can be done without formal leadership, but requires an individual or individuals willing to lead without the formal title. Remember: I never said it would be easy.

I hope that in your work experience, you have examples of working on a team that functioned without a formal manager or with minimal leader involvement except when they were needed. I know that leadership is needed especially for communicating clear goals, priorities, and direction; however, I believe that leadership skills, including emotional intelligence and team-building, can belong to anyone. There is a podcast entitled "How to Have an Effective Team Without a Leader"[4] that discusses what is needed by the team to be effective working together—with or without a leader—and how important communication is considering the amount of time spent communicating when a team is really working together.

I thought about my experiences as a member of several teams and the required elements for effective and cohesive functioning described in Patrick Lencioni's model: building trust, mastering conflict, achieving commitment, embracing accountability, and focusing on results.[5] I shared with you earlier my memories of a small team that worked very hard and achieved good results for our organization in a multiday leadership training event. As I think back I realize that trust built slowly over time and through managing our conflicts, which included testing each other's commitment to the project, delivering on our commitments, working through disagreements and ego, respecting each other's area of expertise, and staying focused on the results. To the credit of the multiple layers of leadership involved, our project vision, goals, and support were clear.

Our first conflicts were uncomfortable, like the first fight with someone that you are in a relationship with. In a good way we were forced to stay together and collaborate because we *needed* each other. We shared leadership/collaboration, from the project leader to the team members; one of us would always pull us back together. Attacks were minimal and not personal. I was reminded of what Lencioni said about team building: It is heavy lifting.

Delegate

Delegation is a key to productive workdays, engagement, and good management; this process and skill requires effective communication.

Typically, delegation is the leader's or manager's action of transferring the responsibility for a task, ongoing activity, or even larger project to a team member. This delegation can be a regular part of daily work or something intended to be developmental for the individual. Project and team leads also delegate work. There are some practical considerations (time, letting go, and trust) and skills that are part of a successful delegation experience for both the delegator and the delegatee. My focus here is on the communication aspect of delegation and I am going to be radical here and suggest that team members delegate to each other.

Why should we delegate? The simple answer is: to get more things done well by freeing up the person who is delegating and in some cases developing and motivating the person who is delegated to. In Chapter 3, on my six-box matrix tool, delegation was an option following an honest answer to the question "Is this work something someone else could or should do?" And remember the exercise in Chapter 4: "If I had more time, I would. . . ." These questions would be very helpful to scenario managers Josh and Donna. Both had opportunities to delegate to people on their teams, but threw away the opportunity to gain more focus and time along with engaging and developing people.

However, our main focus has been on individual contributors who do not have formal authority over other people, so let's talk about delegation for this person. With support from your leader and a collaborative approach to work, peers could delegate to each other.

There are guidelines for effective delegation regardless of whether you have a manager/supervisor/lead title or not:

- ✓ Examine your mindset about delegation and make sure you see delegation as a collaborative tool and not dumping on people.
- ✓ Clearly communicate what you are asking the person to do and the importance of the task,

timeframe, and any parameter like budget, authority, and so on.
✓ Follow up, but with the intention to assist if
needed, not to micromanage.
✓ Have the support of your leader if you do not have
formal authority.

Your communication skills may be tested to ensure the best
outcomes and strong relationships. Especially for team leads
and peers, there is a balance needed between being too directive or too apologetic. Nicole from Scenario 1 sent an abrupt
and directive email to her peers about their responsibilities for
the project she led. Everyone's emotions were already on edge
with their manager's sudden departure and all the unknowns
that followed. Nicole sprang into action and had her project
deadlines and priority validated with the interim executive. I
think that talking with her peers about the project would have
gone a long way before she sent an email reminding them of
their project tasks. Then maybe her actions and email would
not have been perceived as something negative by the team.

I am imagining Nicole saying to me, "Mary, I didn't have
time for that. I am direct and had to get them focused on my
project and shouldn't have to tip-toe around them." I would
agree with her about not having to use time to tip-toe around
peers working for the good of the organization. However, I
would say that taking time to talk with people before she sent
her email about her intentions, especially when emotions are
in play, would have been a good use of her time.

Never underestimate the value of effective communication
on your workday.

Influence/Initiate/Persuade

An essential skill for a good workday is to know how and when
to speak up wisely and professionally in order to influence,

initiate, persuade, and even say no at times. I call this "strategic communication" and it is mandatory for good workdays. What happens under pressure is that people react—leaders, coworkers, customers—and reaction often leads to commands, instructions, and/or directions that are given in haste. In a real emergency, this is needed; we want someone to take charge and give instructions.

But for the many situations that are not true emergencies, there will be the need for people to speak up before jumping up. I give an easy model in Chapter 6. To use this model, we will need to initiate, influence, persuade, and even say no.

Situation

Your manager reacts to an executive inquiry/idea about a feedback tool (you don't know if it was a casual idea or a need surfaced from a board member) and tells you to add this tool to a pilot about to go live. Your manager has reacted and you need to stay calm. You know from experience that although it is a good tool, this is not a quick or easy addition; you know this would require quality communication and coordination for which the timeframe doesn't allow. If you are like me, you just really want to say, "No, no way! This will not work! It's too late! What are you thinking?"

Your communication choices

Reactive

- ✓ Get upset and argue.
- ✓ Try to scramble and rush this new tool into the pilot causing chaos for peers, twenty pilot participants, and about a couple hundred other people.
- ✓ Complain to colleagues about this last-minute request and your lack of autonomy.

✓ Your communication is visibly, vocally, and verbally emotional.

Strategic

✓ Agree with the positive value of the tool (which
   you do see).
✓ Share concerns from a business and customer perspective about rushing this into the pilot and not
   taking the time to do this well (examples: confiden-
   tiality might be at risk; people won't have enough
   time to respond; a poor first experience will leave a
   lasting impression).
✓ Offer the option of putting the tool into the post-
   pilot future programs.
✓ Your communication is visibly, vocally, and verbally positive, confident, open, and professional.

Being strategic will not guarantee you the outcomes you
think are best, but it will build your leadership and confidence.
You spoke up because you cared about the success of the pilot
for the people, customers, your manager, and the organization. You are able to see both risks and benefits to the request.
You had the courage to speak up in a positive way, offering
thoughtful alternatives. Even if the request for the feedback
tool remains, you have done your best to be proactive in your
response. In situations like this I have "won" some and "lost"
some, but I never regretted having the strategic conversation.

In the situation that I gave you, here is some of the strategic
language:

✓ Here is what I/we can do in this timeframe . . .
✓ We could try . . .
✓ I have some concerns about . . .
✓ Help me understand the background on this . . .

Think back to times when you may have done this or times when you wish you or others had.

What about saying no and drawing boundaries with bosses? There are times at work when saying no is the right thing to do. However, in the workday situations that we have been talking about, usually saying no as an emotional reaction is not an option. Imagine if Lucas lost it and vented "Look, the team and I are sick of your midnight and weekend messages; I'm not going to respond until Monday!" or "Why did you volunteer us for all this extra work?" I think a break-up would have been a possibility after these communications.

Here are several examples of a strategic communication for Lucas to set some boundaries with Josh for the benefit of them both:

- ✓ "Josh, I have a serious issue to talk about with you and need some of your time. After work hours and on the weekend, I focus on my family and get reenergized for the work week ahead. I notice that you send out a lot of emails and texts during that time. Let's come up with a plan so that you and I both get our needs met."
- ✓ "Josh, this is what I can do: read and respond to your messages on Sunday evenings."
- ✓ "How about if you used text for anything urgent only."
- ✓ "I need your time to talk for the project because I see some risks for the customer."
- ✓ "I'm interested in what you are looking for in these meetings."

Yes, this would take time and preparation but could make the work relationship so much better for everyone.

Choosing the Best Communication Method

The best choice for difficult conversations is still face-to-face communication. Remember those body language clues that can help us communicate effectively. The next best choice is to talk with someone; the tone of our voices can help us to understand meaning and to convey meaning as a way to reinforce the words—concern, interest, enthusiasm, confusion, and so on.

Email is great for one-way communication, but sometimes these messages need follow-up with a call or a meeting to allow dialogue and connection. Before I send what I think may be an unexpected or challenging email, I sometimes call the recipient first to give them a heads-up. Remember that even email may stir up emotions that impact energy and focus.

It is so easy to misunderstand each other, but at least if we are face-to-face, we can see the visual and vocal clues and get back on the right track. With email we see words on a screen and may read a "tone" where none was intended (maybe the receiver is tired or distracted or overly busy). Or if the sender of the message was upset, tired, distracted, or too busy, maybe they deliberately put in a sarcastic, annoyed tone.

Summary

Communication makeover opportunities for scenario people:

New Communication Strategy	Character	Scenario
Set boundaries	Nicole with peers Jim with Carla Lucas with Josh Donna with her team	1 2 3 4

Escalate	Jim and Carla to manager	2
	Lucas to Josh	3
Collaborate/Lead Collaboration	Nicole with peers	1
	Jim and Carla	2
	Josh and his team	3
	Donna and her team	4
Delegate	Josh to his team	3
	Donna and her team	4
Influence, Persuade	Lucas to Josh	3
	Josh to his boss	3
	Donna to her manager	4

Think about the relationship improvements for the scenario characters if they communicated more effectively. Effective communication is a fundamental and critical skill in all of our relationships—one which can add or destroy work production, creativity, quality, and enjoyment. Communication can build, sustain, or chip away at our workday engagement.

The real power of being a skilled communicator will come from our authenticity. If we come from our honest best self with positive intentions along with using techniques, models, and formulas, the possibilities for improvement and change are real. Here are some reminders as we move on to the next chapter:

- ✓ Establish boundaries, if needed.
- ✓ Your communication with others will impact your workday—for the better or worse.
- ✓ Do not avoid the difficult conversations.
- ✓ Manage technology; respect others' time/style and use it well.
- ✓ Expect conflict and manage it.
- ✓ Monitor your real listening skills.
- ✓ Get some feedback.

✓ Review your communication needs and skills, especially the skill of adapting to improve your communication with others.

Reflection and Action

Reflection

✓ Identify your difficult conversations.
✓ Think about why these are difficult for you:
  ■ Message.
  ■ Emotions—fear, unease, disapproval, disappointment, dislike.
  ■ Reactions—theirs, yours.

✓ Put together your list of difficult conversations:
  ■ Pushing back to influence your manager.
  ■ Asking people to meet deadlines.
  ■ Not wanting to be perceived as whining or not perfect.
  ■ Not saying no.
  ■ Wanting to please.
  ■ Standing up to aggressive people.
  ■ Being honest with team members when you don't agree.

Action

✓ Develop a strategy and language to have one of your difficult conversations.
✓ Practice with a trusted role model.
✓ Have the conversation and learn from what went well and what you will do differently next time.

Confront, Challenge, and Conquer Chaos

Job requirements (continued):

- » Must be ready for anything.
- » Remain calm and thoughtful.
- » Effective communication is critical.
- » Land on your feet.
- » Recognize the glass as half full.
- » Value people and work collaboration.
- » See possibilities for yourself, your team, and your organization.
- » Be accountable and solve problems.
- » A sense of humor goes a long way.
- » High levels of determination, tenacity, energy, and resilience.
- » Dedicated, enthusiastic, and inspired with pride in one's work.

In everyday language "chaos" implies the existence of unpredictable or random behavior. The word usually carries a negative connotation involving undesirable disorganization or confusion. However, in the scientific realm this unpredictable behavior is not necessarily undesirable.[1] Yet even if some workday chaos is desirable, it has to be confronted/challenged to be able to learn and eventually benefit from it. This chapter's focus is on strategies and tools to help manage unnecessary work chaos that has now sneakily become just "routine," expected, and overlooked.

I think that to conquer chaos, we want to first talk about confronting and challenging chaos in order to conquer some of it. To confront means to face, address, and call out rather than ignore, accept, or try to escape. Confronting chaos fits with our central theme of leading ourselves to make the most of our workdays. Once we have confronted it, we can consider other choices and actions: use chaos, learn from chaos, or then reject chaos with different approaches and behaviors. So our starting point needs to be facing chaos, acknowledging it, naming it chaos, and honestly evaluating the results from working continually in a chaotic way.

This is another chapter with which I have some personal and professional history. I learned about chaos theory in graduate school, and I started teaching a course about managing chaos for the American Management Association in the mid-2000s. I began to be part of chaos firsthand when I worked in telecommunications; traveled every week for work to different parts of the United States; worked in the energy industry; and worked in my own business, which has included individuals, teams, and leaders from several federal government agencies along with a wide variety of other organizations. Many people with whom I worked were searching for answers beyond time management courses.

As mentioned, chaos has expanded and is often accepted, expected, and worked around. But work-arounds impact our ability to make the most of our workdays and affect organization growth and success. So why hasn't chaos been confronted and challenged more at the organization, leader, and individual levels? I think the answer can be found by looking at the organization, leadership, and individual levels separately. At the organizational levels, we have to factor in the quantity and complexity of the large changes that impact the external and internal worlds of organizations. Organizations and leaders are grappling with balancing many seemingly opposing concepts: growth versus stability, standardization versus flexibility/innovation, risk versus opportunity, being the employer of choice work versus cuts to compensation and benefits, just to name a very few sources of challenge.

Leaders are part of the organization's struggles and dilemmas and in the position of inspiring and challenging people while managing the fallout from the chaos generated by external sources or top leadership. There is a quote about leadership from a church sign that a manager brought to leadership training. I am paraphrasing the quote here but it was about leaders needing to "rock the boat" without capsizing it! Leaders are managing chaos at multiple levels, which include themselves.

On the individual level, I think that some of the answer is in the fact that change is so hard and that the status quo has a very strong hold on us. Think about it: You know your current chaos and to confront it and propose different approaches will mean behavior changes and more uncertainty with those changes. There is some chaos at work that we cannot conquer, but confronting chaos starting with our circle of control is a step toward minimizing, learning from, and even eliminating and conquering some chaos.

Impact and Results of Chaos

On the organization level, unmanaged chaos can lead to great loss: losing reputation, people, customers, revenue, lawsuits, investments, budget, and stock price. On the leader and individual levels, chaos has a negative effect on workday productivity, satisfaction, and engagement. You can see this reflected in some the low engagement scores, attrition rates, error rates, missed deadlines, and health problems.

One of the worst results of chaos is the uncertainty and the "out of control" feeling that it brings, which is a basic threat to people. David Rock, who wrote *Your Brain at Work*, includes information about the basic threat that uncertainty presents: "Uncertainty is like an inability to create a complete map of a situation, and with parts missing, you're not as comfortable as when the map is complete."[2]

Living with workday uncertainty is not a healthy state for us physically, mentally, or emotionally. The following questions are just a sample of what the workdays present, which chaos can increase and heighten in tension:

- ✓ Will I have enough time to do the job well with these moved-up deadlines?
- ✓ Will my coworker meet my deadline now that he has a new project?
- ✓ Will the team accept me as the lead?
- ✓ Will the new leader give me some control over the strategic plan?
- ✓ Will I get out of here on time to pick up the kids?

These questions are just a sample of the challenges to our feeling somewhat in control at work and are related to the common workday needs in Chapter 1:

- ✓ Wanting to have some control over their work and the workday.
- ✓ Needing clear and achievable work expectations.
- ✓ Having good work relationships with coworkers and colleagues.
- ✓ Having some downtime to refocus, reenergize, and renew.
- ✓ Feeling connected and not being alone with problems.
- ✓ Being somewhere between boredom and unhealthy stress at work.
- ✓ Being treated fairly and contributing honest results to their organization.

Workday chaos at the organization, leader, and individual levels is a threat to everything above with potential ripple effects both within and beyond the organization.

A Word About Good Chaos

It's important to acknowledge that some chaos is good. Stop and think about any good chaos in your life or at work. For me, I think of the unexpected opportunities at work that have come along, the people who popped up in my life and taught me something new by issuing me a challenge, or seeing some new role or path I wanted. Other things included a memorable role model and leader who pushed me out of my comfort zone; writing a book; a culture transformation project with tight implementation resources; and going back to school, seeking a job change, or moving to another state.

I have to remind myself that these happy changes and growth opportunities came with a cost—some chaos, uncertainty, discomfort, and loss of feeling that I was in control. That's helpful to remember since there may be some *good things* hidden in our work chaos: new skill growth, leadership opportunity, and creative thinking to name a few.

"Before" Profile for Josh and Lucas

The scenarios all contain elements of unproductive chaos: change, confusion about leaders, priorities, and misuse of time and people. Let's look at Scenario 3 in more depth since it gives us a look at leadership chaos and the impact on team members.

Josh, a leader of twenty people, was overstretched by the normal workload and still volunteered his team for anything that came up from his boss. There is a new person, Lucas, who was in over his head leading the wrong project. Josh was disorganized and trying all kinds of things for help and rejecting them all. What a mess.

Manage Yourself

- ✓ Josh doesn't see how he is a source of some chaos for his team and himself.
- ✓ Josh doesn't see Lucas's enthusiasm fading and being replaced by disengagement.
- ✓ Lucas is moving from enthusiastic to worry to disengagement.
- ✓ Josh thinks everyone on his team should be like him.
- ✓ Josh's mindset: Just plough through.
- ✓ Lucas's mindset: I should be able to do this.

Focus on Priorities

✓ Josh jumps around from task to task, losing focus.

✓ Josh does not coach or develop his team.

✓ Josh has dropped team meetings.

Value Time and Energy

✓ Josh overcommits his team.

✓ Josh spends most of his time reacting.

✓ Josh doesn't make time to listen to or coach Lucas.

✓ Lucas and Josh are spending too much time at work.

Communicate Effectively

✓ Josh is intimidated by some team members.

✓ Josh is not trying to influence his boss, and his team is now overloaded.

✓ Josh doesn't really listen.

✓ Lucas is now afraid to speak up.

Confront, Challenge, and Conquer Chaos

✓ Josh thinks the chaos is from incompetent staff and being understaffed.

✓ Lucas and team focused on day-to-day survival or planning to leave.

It's Not Me, It's You

A common cry about chaos is "It's not me, it's you" (the boss, coworker, customer, organization); however, the reality is that we probably all have contributed to the chaos and that some chaos is a natural part of changes big and small. In Chapter 4 we talked about a type of day called "I bring the chaos."

Sometimes someone in one of my workshops will say in frustration, "I was sent here by my boss who really needs to be here." That's not a surprise since managers and leaders are individuals facing workday challenges just like everyone else. In addition, they create a team culture that reduces chaos or increases chaos. We have seen several times in this book that interpersonal skills and priorities are often the work that is dropped because these are not recognized as immediately important. However, taking this approach will usually lead to greater problems that catch up with organizations and leaders. Remember the "top priority but not urgent" quadrant in the priority matrix?

Consider how we can unintentionally create some chaos and check off your own experiences for the following "Have you ever" items:

- ✓ Finished some tedious work, needed a break, and popped in to "visit" someone? That's good, right? Relationships are important and necessary. Absolutely, if the timing was right for the person you decided to visit. (A note about generation differences: A person in a class was complaining about the younger generation at work who spend time on social media. A younger coworker laughed noting that the pop-in visitors were not that different from people interrupting each other via text.)
- ✓ Called out to someone in a cubicle environment? (I have to plead guilty to this one.)
- ✓ Spent too much time on a task/project because of your own perfectionism and caused a delay for someone else?
- ✓ Put off starting work on a task/project as part of your procrastination with this particular thing and caused rush problems for someone else?

✓ Didn't speak up and accepted something that impacted your other deadlines and people?

✓ Didn't ask questions to clarify and then had to spend time redoing work?

✓ Didn't take the time to communicate clearly, which caused more emails or visits from people who don't understand what you said or need?

✓ Held on to work that you should have given or trained someone else to do?

You see the chain of impact that can result from any of these common actions. Sometimes we cause chaos for others without thinking. Sometimes we cause chaos for ourselves by not looking ahead to prevent or reduce some chaos. But if you did check off one or more items, multiply that by the "others" and you can see why there is so much chaos at the institutional, unit, leader, and individual levels.

Now, let's take it chapter by chapter to make sure we identify the causes of chaos.

Chapter 2

This chapter was all about you, but most of us are not working alone and impact other people and their workdays. Trying to get our needs met, it's easy to negatively impact others, which in turn impacts the work. Here are some additions to the "Have you ever" list:

✓ Not known when you should not send an email or make a call?

✓ Not managed your mindset or emotions?

✓ Not remained calm, breathed deep, and stepped back when needed?

Chapter 3

This chapter was about understanding and committing to priorities—long-term, proactive ones along with the short-term, in-your-face ones. A huge source of chaos that I see and struggle with personally is to give time and top energy to Box 2 in the priority matrix tool. I see that tendency also at the organization and leader levels. Ironically, not prioritizing things like developing and coaching, planning, cross-training, process improvement on the how we work together level, and/or innovating leads to more urgent crisis situations.

Not anticipating new priorities, resources, and/or delays can cause some chaos that should and could have been *predicted and prepared for.*

Chapter 4

This chapter was about valuing time and energy, and setting aside times to reenergize and times to bring our best focus. That's great, but the people around us also have best and down times, so awareness of this also matters; closed doors, weekends, or vacations don't stop some people from barging in physically or virtually. This chapter also included:

- ✓ Not building in time to unwind.
- ✓ Not managing distractions.
- ✓ Setting meetings without clear purpose and value.
- ✓ Not setting meetings that are needed.

Chapter 5

This chapter focused on effective communication and on managing conflict as a necessity. This has to include not only effective verbal communication but also written communication. This includes communication not only to your manager but also to your coworkers and everyone else.

✓ Not sharing information with everyone about work on teams and between teams, departments, and so on leads to confusion, redundancy, and interpersonal and process conflict.

✓ Failing to speak up, strategically push back and escalate when needed.

✓ Sending hurried emails that are confusing or sarcastic.

✓ Spitting out emails without thinking to whom they should really go.

✓ Not delegating effectively with clear communication, conversation, process, and follow-up.

Strategies and Tools

1. Head Off Chaos

Application Tool: Anticipating and Preparing

I don't think we could or even want to prepare for all the unexpected things, but let's be honest: There are some patterns to the chaos that we could get a jump on. What I am talking about are the things that repeat and cause confusion and distress, yet we just continue to go along in the same way.

So it is a great strategy to anticipate and prepare for the unexpected when we are able to. Here are some patterns and trends to start you off:

✓ People at work get sick; families get sick.

✓ Things take longer to complete than we often realize or communicate.

✓ Some people are not known for their clear communication or expectations.
✓ Walk-in interruptions or welcome (or unwelcome)
   distractions happen at certain times with certain
   people.
✓ New major initiatives can come at the drop of a
   hat.
✓ Customers may be crabbier on the return line, the
   help line, or the "we close soon" line.

If you take some time, you can add to this list based on
your workdays and life. If some planning has gone by the
wayside in these chaotic workplaces and workdays, you can
imagine how this chapter's concept will really be under fire.
We don't have time! Being proactive means thinking about the
trends and then doing something about them.

Thinking about work, I tried to think about when I could
have or did plan for the unexpected.

✓ Knowing beforehand that in certain meetings I
   had to control my feelings because of past confron-
   tations and reactions.
✓ Cross-training people to do what I did in case I
   was not around.
✓ Encouraging others to cross-train and line up
   people as back up.
✓ Anticipating extra review time for a very detail-
   oriented manager.
✓ Learning something new in case I had to step in.
✓ Paying attention to my/team's Box 2.
✓ Predicting problems and having a Plan B.
✓ Realistic promising in order to deliver or over deliver.
✓ Building in time cushions where I could for unex-
   pected delays.

✓ Managing expectations (my own, my team's, my customers', or my manager's).

2. Watch Your Initial Reaction When Chaos Comes

Application Tool: Basic Chaos Model

1. Stop.
2. Stay cool and calm under pressure; manage emotions.
3. Think before reacting.

Often in chaotic situations, we spring into a reaction, and sometimes that action can cause even more chaos. I understand that there isn't a lot of time to stop and think, but even a very brief pause before reacting can be very beneficial. However, we have to stop and stay calm in order to think. "Your ability to regulate your emotions instead of being at the mercy of them is central to being effective in a chaotic world."[3]

In Chapter 3, remaining calm was discussed as a necessity when priorities change and compete. Here it is again as critical to confronting any type of chaos. Has this type of chaos ever happened to you? You are blindsided by someone forgetting to tell you about a big change that directly impacts an internal or external customer presentation the next day. As a result, you have to scramble that night, change your plan, and study new content so that you can be well prepared for your customers. If you had any plans to do other work or to do something personal, that plan is out. You have some choices in your initial reactions: get upset and angry; recognize that your understandable initial reaction needs to be managed first by breathing, then by thinking; figure out how to best manage the situation for the customers; and consider any possible resources. You followed the basic model above, however, there are more options to consider if you want to confront and conquer this type of chaos. There is communication to find out what happened to cause this error or oversight (not in a blaming way but in a positive problem-solving way) and the impacts on everyone involved. To go even further, problem- or chaos-solving can include a session to figure out how to prevent future chaos like this. Now I see that positive warrior approach in action rather than not following up.

3. Think Before Reacting—Respond With Resources and Skills

Application Tool: Skills

- ✓ Stay in the "calm" zone and with a positive mindset.
- ✓ Brainstorm and collaborate ideas and options— visual tools are fast and effective.
- ✓ Innovate and create new options or ways of doing things.
- ✓ Communicate strategically your/your team's ideas and options.
- ✓ Negotiate.
- ✓ Manage expectations.
- ✓ Reframe and find some benefits in the situation.
- ✓ Adapt and be resilient.

———

There are several tools from quality and process improvement, problem-solving, and even creativity workshops that can be fast and effective ways to brainstorm, analyze, and come up with options for managing chaos. The American Management Association courses contain many of these tools; you can also use the Mind Tools website (*www.mindtools.com*) to find a collection of these tools. You may find that you are using them in other areas in your organization.

———

You will need the strategic communication skills and tools discussed in Chapter 5. Let's see this in action. What if your boss is the source of some major chaos? Instead of ignoring and suffering, as Josh's team does in Scenario 3, you have some other choices and strategies.

- ✓ Our supervisors and managers can bring chaos, that is, trickle-down chaos.
- ✓ Ineffective meetings, poorly run, too long, do not meet purpose.
- ✓ Not using team meetings for problem-solving or collaboration.
- ✓ Not managing performance consistently and fairly.
- ✓ Too busy to give feedback.
- ✓ Passing on emails without clarifying action and response.
- ✓ Unclear communication.
- ✓ Dumping instead of effective delegation.
- ✓ Micromanaging, adding to the workloads.
- ✓ Leaders who don't have strategic communication skills with their peers and leaders.
- ✓ Someone has to try and stop some chaos; if you are reading this book, that's you.

Have a strategic conversation around making things better and problem-solving, not the blame game of pointing your finger at them, which will push most of us into defensiveness and also possibly put us at risk with our manager.

- ✓ Share tools from a class, article, or book.
- ✓ Bring suggestions and ideas, not just problems and complaints.
- ✓ Volunteer first to try an idea or tool at the next meeting.

Here are some samples of strategic language, both what to say and what not to say.

What to Say

- ✓ I'm interested in what you need from me/us with these new reports.
- ✓ I have an idea how we could work together more effectively.
- ✓ Yes, I/we can add that project and need your help with reprioritizing my other work.
- ✓ I need some clarity about this assignment and have organized my questions; when do you have time to talk (persistence will be needed)?
- ✓ I have some suggestions for the team meetings and volunteer to set up team brainstorming at our next meeting. We'll need about thirty minutes.
- ✓ I'd like to set a time for some feedback about my work, which will help me in moving forward correctly.

What Not to Say

- ✓ What I'd really like to say is. . . ! (You can fill this in yourself!)

Here are some ideas for a general team "chaos prevention" meeting including virtual meetings:

- ✓ Come up with a way for people to connect as people even if only briefly (fun, telling a joke, music, and so on).
- ✓ Share positive news, feedback, and recognition.
- ✓ Review the team matrix.
- ✓ Establish a team "surveillance" and discuss news/things on the horizon that will impact the team.

✓ Make collaboration requests or specific plans, not vague plans.

✓ Making sure not to get lost in detail that is not pertinent to all.

✓ People should leave feeling and thinking that they were engaged in this team meeting and that the meeting was worth their time.

All of these need to be accompanied by a professional, positive tone of voice and confident body language along with the words. Don't forget about the importance of timing and that your own leader has a perspective and challenges that you are not always aware of.

Stuff Happens

I was on a team of about eight people. We had solo and also joint projects that involved scheduling large but limited meeting rooms, scarce dates, and invitations to internal and external customers. This was pretty complicated with lots of moving parts and a very important part of the projects. When this part was done, everyone on the project team sighed in relief. Usually these were commitments for the year's calendar.

For some reason, one of the project leaders had to change a date (probably an external pressure) and wanted the large conference room my project team had already reserved. The pressure was on to give up the room for the other project and for us to find another room (not so easy for us).

The first reactions on both teams were: "Well, you will have to change your dates or room; my project is the high priority." The scene reminded me of a standoff in a Western movie between the good and bad guys, except that we were both the good guys. Here we go again; remember Chapter 3. We were set in the silo cement until we actually drew out on a whiteboard an "Ours" matrix for the team. Both projects were top priorities, but my peer's project had the "urgent" criteria since it was scheduled to happen sooner.

However, brainstorming showed that their one-day event contrasted our three-day event and that the cost of relocating us to a hotel was too high. In the end, my peer had to book a hotel.

Some changes bring normal chaos; we had to move to objective problem-solving as soon as we could get beyond "That's too bad, we got there first."

You cannot shortchange communication even in chaotic times. Sometimes there may be things that go beyond this book's focus on good workdays and the need to communicate and escalate could be mandatory.

- ✓ If inappropriate behaviors are exhibited by anyone, you may need help from human resources, leaders, or ethics hot lines.
- ✓ Witnessing or participating in harmful gossip.
- ✓ Mistreating or witnessing mistreatment.

The Connection of Saying No, Distractions, and Workload

I came across an article entitled "Signs that You're a Pushover," which contained some good workday advice. Part of the strategic communication presented in Chapter 5 included how not speaking up to persuade and say no at times can lead to chaos for yourself and others. One of the strategies that the author shares in this article is learning to say no graciously: "If you are easily persuaded by others, chances are that it shows up in your calendar. How often are you being persuaded to attend a meeting or change your schedule to accommodate the needs of others? Never say yes or no in the moment."[4]

Lacking the strategic communication skills of persuasion and influencing others may be adding to our workload and schedule. I realize that most of us are not always in a position to say no, but we can use the article's technique when we are. There are times, however, when we can say no; both Nicole in Scenario 1 and Donna in Scenario 4 created some of their own chaos by not saying no graciously to requests and interruptions. But again, you would have to 1) give yourself permission to say no sometimes; 2) use the right language; and 3) build up and practice your skills.

Let's come back to Scenario 3 and look at options for Josh and Lucas. Josh was the somewhat chaotic manager who did not have a clue about what his team was feeling or considering. And Lucas was the enthusiastic new team member who was becoming demotivated very fast.

"After" Profile for Josh and Lucas

Manage Yourself

- ✓ Josh doesn't see how he is a source of some chaos for his team and himself.
- ✓ Josh doesn't see Lucas's enthusiasm fading and being replaced by disengagement.
- ✓ Lucas is moving from enthusiastic to worry to disengagement.
- ✓ Josh thinks everyone on his team should be like him.
  - *Josh gets or seeks some feedback from his team.*
  - *Josh's new mindset: acknowledges to himself that he is a new leader and needs some help.*
  - *Lucas's new mindset: Decides not give up yet because he wanted this job; he will try other things before leaving.*

Focus on Priorities

- ✓ Josh jumps around from task to task, losing focus.
- ✓ Josh does not coach or develop his team.
- ✓ Josh has dropped team meetings.
  - ■ *Lucas or Josh make a positive case for the value of team meetings; suggest team involvement to redesign an agenda.*
  - ■ *Team talks about using a team matrix so everyone can see the priorities and resources.*

Value Time and Energy

- ✓ Josh overcommits his team.
- ✓ Josh spends most of his time reacting.
- ✓ Josh doesn't make time to listen to or coach Lucas.
- ✓ Lucas and Josh are spending too much time at work.
  - ■ *Josh stops volunteering his team without considering the workload, talking to them.*
  - ■ *Lucas establishes a boundary with Josh about twenty-four-seven email responses on nonurgent matters and problem-solves to develop a plan with Josh to get what he needs for anything urgent versus waiting until Monday or the next shift.*

Communicate Effectively

- ✓ Josh is intimidated by some team members.
- ✓ Josh is not trying to influence his boss and his team is now overloaded.
- ✓ Josh doesn't really listen.
- ✓ Lucas is now afraid to speak up.
  - ■ *Lucas tells Josh about his deep concerns regarding the project role and what would help.*

- *Josh considers making a case to his boss about resources (even if temporary).*
- *Josh holds a team lunch as a "thank you" and opens up for feedback.*

Confront, Challenge, and Conquer Chaos

✓ Josh thinks the chaos is from incompetent staff and being understaffed.

✓ Lucas and some of the team focused on day-to-day survival.

- *Josh looks at team burnout and his own burnout and draws boundaries for everyone in terms of their time at work, after-hours spent on work, and true urgency.*
- *Team brings suggestions for how they could work with more collaboration.*

Resiliency, Change, and Chaos

We've been considering how to confront, challenge, and conquer some chaos. Some of that chaos comes from ongoing changes, usually coming very fast and with more levels of complexity in many workplaces.

Resiliency is an ability, skill, and characteristic that needs to be added to our list of resources. What is resiliency? The ability to rebound quickly from a crisis or a trauma.[5]

Here is some great news about this critical ability: Leadership skills, including, resilience can be learned even though scientists agree there is some genetic component. "Yet, like almost any behavior, resilience can also be learned," says Goldstein, a psychologist at the University of Utah. "In fact, research shows that resilient people share some common qualities—ones you can cultivate to master any crisis."[6]

Here are some things to help us develop more resilience:

- ✓ A resilient mindset sees opportunity, not problems that cannot be solved.
- ✓ Positive relationships, health, and optimism.
- ✓ Identifying what is stable in your life—internal things like your values.
- ✓ Reminding yourself of what skills and approaches you have used in the past to manage disruption, tough times, and change. (Reflecting on every member's strengths to manage surprises and adversity might be a good team activity.)
- ✓ Anticipate change when you can.
- ✓ See opportunity along with loss.

Summary

Because this has been my area of immersion officially since 2005 (and experiencing chaos unofficially since the 1990s), I want to acknowledge some concerns about chaos's impact on the workday:

- ✓ Chaos is growing at work, in some homes, communities, and general cultures.
- ✓ We often don't solve problems for the long run; we just react, move on, and things get worse.
- ✓ Work relationships are sacrificed, even though as human beings we need good relationships at work.
- ✓ Health and wellness may be at risk.

People are too busy to read emails, instructions, or do what they are supposed to do. We are losing a sense of accountability, sometimes not seeing ourselves honestly and what we owe to the organization and team. "I need an exception; I am going to meetings all the time and don't have time to give you what we agreed."

To go back to comparing our engagement at work with a personal relationship, every relationship needs some good chaos, but too much of the negative kind will have a serious cost and may even lead to a bad break-up. Take the time to see, confront, challenge, and conquer some unnecessary chaos—and please don't accept it as inevitable.

Reflection and Action

Reflection

- ✓ What are your biggest sources of chaos?
  - ■ From others:
  - ■ That you bring yourself:
- ✓ Think about the resiliency skills that you have used in the past.
- ✓ Decide if you need to build up your resiliency skills.

Action

- ✓ Pick out one source of chaos from others and put down some ideas to address it.
- ✓ Pick out one source of chaos that you bring and put down some ideas to address it.

Choosing Change

Last Job Requirement:

⌃ Change is good; you go first.

I began this book hoping that *hope* would be your catalyst for seizing opportunities and controlling of your workday. Congratulations! You took some time to read this book, took some action, and hopefully found something of value. My goal in this last chapter is to bring us back to the beginning framework so that the roadmap for workday happiness is a springboard forward.

Remember, our engagement with our work is like any relationship: Hard work is required to sustain it, some days are better than others, change and compromise are required, and sometimes you move on amicably as it may not be meant to last forever! I wonder what happened to those three enthusiastic people from Chapter 1 who were new to their jobs and who were so happy just to be working.

I never saw them again. As the 2017 holiday grew in frenzy and impatience and things went wrong with customers, coworkers, managers, and life, how did they handle it and did they sustain their initial engagement? Or maybe they found different jobs or maybe they had to stay where they were because they needed that income, location, and/or whatever benefited them.

I don't know if you were like these three people when you started out in your current job, role, or career. As I think back I remember sometimes being like them and sometimes taking a job because I needed the income and knew deep down that the job and I were not a match. I maintain that it was still up to me to engage and bring my best self to work. Sometimes I succeeded; sometimes not.

Your "Before" profile/current work profile can be the starting point right now. It's your turn for a "Before" and "After" profile and it is your own scenario and your own reality. Each chapter had "Reflection and Action" suggestions at the end; it's helpful now to go back to these for any insights or ideas.

Your "Before"/Current Work Profile

An important step is to both think about and actually write things down about your current situation. You can use these guided reflections to develop a picture of your situation. Reflect and consider:

1. My current job/role is a:
   - Dream job.
   - Stopgap.

- Stepping stone.
- Springboard.
- Other.

2. Relationship phase:
   - Honeymoon.
   - Honeymoon is over, now faced with reality.
   - Need some help to try new things.
   - We can work it out.
   - Time to prepare to move on.
   - Other.

3. What would you like to improve?
   - Your engagement.
   - Your productivity.
   - Your work satisfaction.

4. Current assessment.
   - Your gains from work.
   - Your productivity challenges.
   - Your sources of chaos.
   - Your major dissatisfactions.

Relationships Need Roadmaps

The realities that are part of this book—in the examples, scenarios, and stories—can be pretty harsh and at the same time are realities that many of us face. I want to share a *big secret*: You are the leader of yourself and do not need a special title. This book's roadmap is intended to provoke insights, challenges, and ideas for you to act upon to improve your workday. However, there is still a lot of work for each person who wants a good workday. There is no magic to changing your boss's micromanaging style, your email volume, coworkers' personalities, or department confusion. But, there are actions that can make things better.

Remember the list from Chapter 1 in which we identified some of our common workday hopes and needs:

- ✓ Wanting to have some control over our work and the workday.
- ✓ Needing clear and achievable work expectations.
- ✓ Having good work relationships with coworkers and colleagues.
- ✓ Having some downtime to refocus, re-energize, and renew.
- ✓ Feeling connected and not being alone with problems.
- ✓ Being somewhere between boredom and unhealthy stress at work.
- ✓ Being treated fairly and contributing honest results to our organization.

I look at this list and hope you see what I see: that it is possible to go get what you need instead of waiting for answers, improvements, and positive changes to come to you. Figure out what you need (test for reasonableness) and what is within your influence, and go get it: feedback about how you are doing; clarity about goals, resources, and deadlines; more respectful treatment; or a new job.

The title of a magazine article attracted me when I was in line at Whole Foods: "How to Love Your Job Again When All You Want to Do Is Quit." It continued, "A recent report . . . found that less than 50 percent of workers are satisfied with their jobs."[1]

Even though you can change jobs and that could be the right path, you don't want to change jobs and find yourself facing the same challenges. The article lists eight ways to fall back in love with your current job; some of these actions are the same ones we looked at in depth. But the last action that the author suggests is:

> Feeling powerless is a common cause of worker dissatisfaction. Remind yourself . . . , you always have the power to quit . . . ; you simply choose not to exercise the power for now.[2]

This is a great mindset to take with you. And here's another benefit about falling in love with your job again: Even if you decide someday to leave your current role or organization, chances are strong that you will find similar problems in the new department, team, organization, and in yourself. The roadmap contains strategies and tools that will be part of your success and happiness wherever you work and whatever you do.

A Good Roadmap Workout

Before you use the roadmap for your "After" profile, I have another person to tell you about. I will never forget her from one of the workshops. She knew herself, her role priorities, was active in problem-solving, valued her time and energy, and was a skilled communicator who confronted and proactively conquered chaos.

Let me put you in a situation similar to the one she was experiencing when I met her. Imagine you are an administrative professional supporting an executive at a large scientific research organization and imagine the responsibilities, details, volume and importance of emails, conversations, arrangements, meetings, reports, and conferences that you have to track each day.

However, your work space is located close to the large printing center (you have your own copier and printer). Every quarter, large numbers of new employees—a new hire cohort—would arrive, for the most part young and enthused to be working in your organization and the culture greets them warmly each year.

These new employees, who are working in an office environment perhaps for the first time, have different personalities and seem to assume that you, because you are nearby and in an administrative role, are the one to go to for printer/copier problems. There are instructions and a help desk number posted, but most people want immediate help in the form of another person taking care of the situation.

Now, see and feel the chaos of a string of interruptions each day when the various newcomers run into problems. Constant disruptions all day long make it hard for you to get back to focusing on your work along with sapping your energy.

David Rock's book *Your Brain at Work* has compelling information about the need to manage external distractions. "The challenge is that any distraction however small diverts your attention. It then takes effort to shift your attention back to where it was before the distraction."[3] The person I am telling you about must have known about "how much energy is involved in high-level thinking such as planning and creating,"[4] which was an important part of her executive support role. So what would you do? You could:

- ✓ Get angry, grumble, and complain to other people, blaming the interrupters for any work delays or lack of quality in your work.
- ✓ Complain to your executive.
- ✓ Suffer constant interruptions to your day.
- ✓ Use your power/status to tell them you don't work for them.

What is your solution?

- ✓ Take some time to think about what you would do and how you would feel and react.

Here's what our example employee did: She knew her priorities and need for focus and that the natural challenge of her cubicle's location would bring constant interruptions. So, she developed a plan and obtained support from her leader.

She greeted each new employee warmly, introduced herself, and told them that she gave each person one "printer orientation" and that after that they were on their own. Problems still came up, but here's where her follow-through and strength kicked in. She did not jump up when new employees came back to her with their copying or printer problems. She was friendly and professional and said she needed to continue with her work; she reminded them that there was a help number posted in the print center. She said this in a confident and friendly way.

Individuals either called the help desk or asked another person for help. Now new employees were interrupting each other and guess what? Peer pressure kicked in and peers set the expectation for each other to learn to become independent with printing needs. They didn't want to be interrupted either.

The point of this exercise is that this person, who was extremely busy with her own responsibilities, came up with a proactive, long-term solution to cut down on some chaos for herself and others. She:

- ✓ Knew the importance of her role, focus, priorities, time, and energy.
- ✓ Welcomed and extended long-term help to new employees by showing them how to be independent.
- ✓ Was an assertive and strategic communicator.
- ✓ Confidently and pleasantly kept to her plan of not taking on printing responsibilities for new employees.

✓ Developed a plan to prevent chaos for herself and others.

This is informal leadership in action and is a determined mindset that anyone can adopt. I share this with you hopefully to inspire you to develop a plan to move forward from your "Before" profile to a new "After" profile.

Your "After"/Desired Profile

Review your "Before" profile and visualize what you would like to see changed in three to six months from now. Each chapter had "Reflection" and "Action" suggestions at the end; go back to and review these for any insights or ideas. Imagine your desired situation:

1. My job/role is a:
   - Dream job
   - Stop gap
   - Stepping stone
   - Springboard
   - Other
2. Relationship phase:
   - Honeymoon.
   - Honeymoon is over, now faced with reality.
   - Need some help to try new things.
   - We can work it out.
   - Time to prepare to move on.
   - Other.
3. Decide how high you want these workday qualities to be:
   - Your engagement:
   - Your productivity:
   - Your work satisfaction:

4. Desired state.
   - Your gains from work.
   - Your productivity challenges within your control.
   - The sources of chaos that you are under your control.
   - How you will address your workday dissatisfactions (the ones under your control and the ones outside of your direct influence).

Next comes what may be the hardest part: What will you do and how will you do it? Will you choose to change anything to reach your desired workday profile?

Change Is Good, Right?

There's something about personal change, and a t-shirt with a Dilbert cartoon summed it up well. The front said, "Change is good," but the back of shirt said, "You go first." I go back to my own words in the Introduction because accompanying the roadmap, the scenarios, strategies, research, and tools is the fundamental challenge of seeking the quantum change that Stephen Covey wrote about.

As you read the scenarios and considered the approaches and ideas, you may have thought, "Why don't they just stop or start or change the way they act?" If you think about it, when you are in your own workday scenarios, is it easy to change your beliefs, thinking, and/or reactions? We may have experienced a challenge anytime we have tried to form a new habit, learn something new, or struggled to stop doing something.

So if there is a strategy, tool, skill, or idea that you want to try, it may not be easy for you to change and also for others who work with you. People will react and your "new way" may be tested, rejected, or even sabotaged before what you are trying can be established. I have heard many times from many workshop participants about how hard it is for them to be assertive, to say no, or change something they already know would make their workday better. Think about it: You probably already knew some or all of the strategies and tools from the roadmap. I think that it is putting these things into the workday that is the hardest part. A wake-up call is needed and even then it may not be enough, as you see from this research.

Even dramatic events are not necessarily wake-up calls but these can be the start we are going to discuss in the next section. In his book *Your Brain at Work*, David Rock says, "A study found that only one in nine people who underwent heart surgery were able to change their lifestyle, and these people had the ultimate 'motivation': possible death."[5]

The Wake-up Call

We need some kind of a starting point, sometimes called an "aha moment"; the insight that is like a wake-up call. I shared one of my moments with you when I wrote about my Saturday morning and tension at a copying/shipping center. Grumbling as I walked along, it hit me that I had this workday in front of me and I was so negative even though this was work I sought and had dreamed about. David Rock describes what happened to me:

> Insights also come with an energetic punch. You can see it on people's faces, hear it in their voices, and see it in their body language. You can even sense it during a telephone call. It's obvious when you know what to listen for. An insight is a moment when things change.[6]

The insight is exciting and gives us energy, desire, and motivation, which we will need for the challenge of whatever it is we want to change, add, stop, try out, improve, accomplish, or learn. We have to get fed up enough, dissatisfied enough, excited enough, or even shocked by a photo, feedback, or someone's (from our family or workplace) reaction to us; that we change our ways of seeing things, shift our perspective, and see something else for ourselves.

The wake-up call can be sudden like it was for me that Saturday morning, or it can be a gradual building up to a change. Maybe you are tired of coming home upset from work every day to brood and not really leave it behind, and you realize that you have another choice. Just the act of realizing that you have a choice is a positive shift toward something else. At least you got off the couch, maybe got angry at tossing away workday time to interruptions, went to a ballgame, or thought about your résumé update!

Action

The wake-up call needs to lead us to action; however, if we want true new results from these new actions, we need to connect our actions with our beliefs, goals, and mindsets.

Remember the actions that were suggested at the end of Chapter 2:

- ✓ Take or review a personality assessment.
- ✓ Establish or review your long-term goals and dreams.
- ✓ Seek feedback to increase your self-awareness and emotional intelligence.
- ✓ Develop your own positive mindset.
- ✓ Have a good talk with yourself every day, at the beginning, during the day, and at the end.

Some of these suggestions are easier than others because we will need to question, challenge, and move out of our comfort zone. That comfort zone is cozy and also has a strong pull for many people. That comfort place is also usually feedback free so there is no danger of getting defensive or threatened by information we don't like or really want. I know people who have taken various personality assessments and feedback tools and then tossed them in the trash. Okay, a superficial action won't do much to change your workday.

I have seen, taken, and facilitated many good tools through my work with customers: personality, teamwork, conflict management, leadership styles, 360-degree feedback, and so on. Two people take a personality or team player assessment. One person looks at his or her results and thinks there's something interesting, files it, or tosses it away. Another person looks at his or her results, is annoyed with something, curious about something, and seeks more information. This person may actually end up using the results to improve his or her communication and work relationships. That is exciting to see and hear someone get an insight from an initial annoyance, cringe, or curiosity about how others see them.

I remember one person in particular who looked at her team player results and told me she was not happy with the results. She began to blame the tool, the research, and me; I remember making neutral comments about viewing any assessment tool results as data for our consideration. The next day, she came up to me and said she was still not happy and intended to change the way others perceived her at work. She stands out positively in my experience with many people as someone who was going to take her unhappiness and dissatisfaction as a catalyst to move to action.

Understanding the need and benefits of workday change are not enough; understanding is not the same as doing. A

2016 *Psychology Today* article states, "If you've ever read a self-help book or article, understood the message, and yet skipped over the exercises, you know exactly what I mean. This is the equivalent of going to the gym and having someone explain how to use a treadmill but then never getting on it."[7]

I appreciate the author's image of learning about the treadmill but not using one; I work with many people who would like to change their behavior and learn skills from a course or through reading. Although these are good starts to increase knowledge and understanding, the new skills usually come from practice, encouraging and helpful coaching, and doing it again and again. Not only do we have to act but also struggle against gravity's pull.

Gravity Pull

You know that when we try to change at the individual, team, and organizational level, there is a natural force cheering and pulling for the status quo. Established habits, routines, and expectations are powerful forces that can seem safe, non-threatening, steady, reliable, "tried and true." So even positive changes for the better—to reduce chaos, innovate, branch out—will require persistence, help, and management.

Earlier I wrote about a challenge of change, that not only do we have to manage our own change but that others (who have their own need for certainty and gravity pull) would probably push back against us. Several powerful forces make up this very human resistance to change:

- ✓ Some beliefs and habits are deeply embedded.
- ✓ Concerns and fears may be valid.
- ✓ We don't all have the same perspective, experience, or information.
- ✓ We have a need for certainty, a need to know what to expect.

✓ Emotions are involved.

✓ Change requires good communication, reinforce-
ment, and renewal.

Since forces are in place to maintain the status quo, what
can you do?

✓ Set goals toward dreams that you really want.

✓ Look forward, imagine, and visualize the benefits
of your changes.

✓ Establish some new realistic habits and routines.

✓ Stay aware of your emotions and emotions of other
people.

✓ Tell your coworkers (and family) what you are
doing and why.

✓ Get some encouraging and supportive people
around you.

✓ See yourself as a resilient, determined, and positive
workday warrior.

✓ Remind yourself of your past success with making
changes.

Keep learning and read further into the resources I've used
in this book and ones that I haven't mentioned—Stephen Covey's
and David Rock's works in particular have made a great impact
on me and helped me to change some beliefs and habits.

I want to leave you with what I think is very good news
from Stephen Covey: "Whatever your present situation, I
assure you that you are not your habits."[8]

Your Action Plan and Next Steps

Think about your "Before"/current workday profile and compare it to your "After"/desired workday profile. The roadmap
we have used can help to close the gap between your current

situation and your desired workday. You can reflect on each roadmap section acknowledging both your strengths and areas to improve or build.

Manage Yourself

✓ Your strengths:
✓ Your areas to improve or build:

Focus on Priorities

✓ Your strengths:
✓ Your areas to improve or build:

Value Time and Energy

✓ Your strengths:
✓ Your areas to improve or build:

Communicate Effectively

✓ Your strengths:
✓ Your areas to improve or build:

Confront, Challenge, and Conquer Chaos

✓ Your strengths:
✓ Your areas to improve or build:

Choosing Change

✓ Your strengths:
✓ Your areas to improve or build:

Next, choose your top three most urgent areas to improve or build.

Considering the first and second parts of this action plan select your top three most pressing challenges related to your engagement, productivity, satisfaction, and overall workday happiness and list what you will do to meet these challenges.

Pressing challenge 1:
Actions:
Pressing challenge 2:
Actions:
Pressing challenge 3:
Actions:

Lastly, identify helpful resources and mindset:

✓ Identify your resources and support (examples: feedback, coaches, sounding boards):
✓ Describe the mindset (and your strengths) that will help you to accomplish your goals in this action plan:

A note about making action plans: It's best to be realistic along with reaching for improvements, especially as you go back to your chaotic workdays. The following are some examples of actions to meet pressing challenges that negatively impact the workday:

✓ Take a course in a certificate program as another step forward.
✓ Walk more; consider health and wellness.
✓ Have lunch with colleagues regularly to improve your work relationships.
✓ Acknowledge what you do get from your work and organization.
✓ Be honest about what you do contribute in work quality, and attitude.
✓ Look at your productivity challenges from the lens of problem-solving.
✓ Addressing your pressing challenges can lead to opportunities that you can't see right now.

Summary

Remember: Change is necessary if you want to make the most of your workday. I want to share some general observations from working with many people that also match my own experiences.

- ✓ Knowing what makes you happy (including family needs) and walking in that direction.
- ✓ Knowing how and when to speak up, push back, offer options, and draw a boundary.
- ✓ Shifting your mindset; you can go home tired by happy even from a crazy, chaotic workday.
- ✓ Making peace with, respecting, and enjoying time. I prefer a river image to the clock face—a river that is moving along with interesting stops along the banks and some rapids that bring not only excitement but learning, danger, and problems to solve.
- ✓ Not forgetting about the people.
- ✓ Getting some help, encouragement, cheering, and feedback because change is hard.
- ✓ Knowing that the workday holds opportunities you may not see.

There is power in numbers. First, look at your workday and make it better; and also get with a group of people and see what you can do collectively. There is even more power when effective strategies, tools, and language are shared and practiced by teams. (Now I will use the word "team" instead of the word "group" since doing this signifies that that the group has grown or transformed into a team.)

I still believe that each workday is precious and filled with opportunities. I have had many work relationships and share with you that I have been in mismatched stopgap jobs, frustratingly slow stepping-stone roles, a springboard job that didn't propel me to where I wanted to go, and a dream job that had its own challenges; I have found that the big contributors to my happiness in all of these places were hope, change, and leading myself.

I wish you all the best ahead with your current work relationship and in all to come.

Now, go make the most of your workday!

NOTES

Introduction

1. Stephen Covey, *The 7 Habits of Highly Effective People* (New York: Free Press, 1989), 31.

Chapter 1

1. Simon Sinek, *Why: How Great Leaders Inspire Everyone to Take Action* (New York: Portfolio, 2009), 7.
2. Ken Royal and Susan Sorenson, "Employees Are Responsible for Their Engagement Too," Gallup, June 16, 2015, *www.gallup.com/businessjournal/183614/employees-responsible-engagement.aspx?g_source=employees+are+responsible+for+their+engagement+too&g_medium=search&g_campaign=tiles*
3. Ibid.
4. Stephen Covey, *The 7 Habits of Highly Effective People* (New York: Free Press, an imprint of Simon & Schuster, 1989), 85.
5. Ibid., 86.

Chapter 2

1. Daniel Goleman, "What Makes a Leader?" in *On Emotional Intelligence* (Boston, MA: HBR Press, 2015), 7.
2. Ben Dattner, "Most Conflicts Aren't Due to Personality," *Harvard Business Review*, May 20, 2014, 4.
3. Daniel Goleman, author website, October 4, 2015, *www.danielgoleman.info/daniel-goleman-how-self-awareness-impacts-your-work/*
4. Royal and Sorenson, "Employees Are Responsible for Their Engagement Too."
5. Dan Pink, *The Puzzle of Motivation*, TEDGlobal 2009, *www.ted.com/talks/dan_pink_on_motivation#t-9767*.

6. Jay M. Jackman and Myra H. Strober, "Fear of Feedback" in *On Emotional Intelligence* (Boston, MA: HBR Press, 2015), 128.
7. Ibid., 127.
8. Sherrie Campbell, "7 Mindsets That Guarantee Enduring Success," *Entrepreneur,* May 5, 2017, *www.entrepreneur.com/article/275149.*

Chapter 3

1. Maura Thomas, "Time Management Training Doesn't Work," *Harvard Business Review,* April 22, 2015.
2. Partners In Leadership, "Getting Key Results Right," March 26, 2015, *www.partnersinleadership.com/insights-publications/getting-key-results-right/*
3. Mind Tools, "Prioritization: Making Best Use of Your Time and Resources," *www.mindtools.com/pages/article/newHTE_92.htm*
4. Patrick Lencioni, *Overcoming the Five Dysfunctions of a Team* (San Francisco, CA: Jossey-Bass, 2005), 69.
5. Ibid., 75.
6. Haig Kouyoumdjian, "Learning Through Visuals: Visual Imagery in the Classroom," *Psychology Today,* July 20, 2012, *www.psychologytoday.com/blog/get-psyched/201207/learning-through-visuals.*
7. Michael Lombardo and Robert Eichinger, *FYI: For Your Improvement, A Guide for Development and Coaching* (Minneapolis, MN: Lominger International, 1996–2009), 63.
8. Patricia Pullam Phillips, Jack J. Phillips, and Rebecca Ray, *Measuring the Success of Employee Engagement* (Alexandria, VA: ATD Press, 2016), 140.

Chapter 4

1. Matthew Kelly, *Resisting Happiness* (North Palm Beach, FL: Beacon Publishing, 2016), 45.
2. Tony Schwartz and Catherine McCarthy, "Manage Your Energy, Not Your Time," *Harvard Business Review,* Winter 2007, 27.
3. Josh Davis, *Two Awesome Hours* (New York: HarperCollins, 2015), 12.
4. Ibid.
5. Ibid., 50.
6. Schwartz and McCarthy, "Manage Your Energy, Not Your Time," 40.
7. David Rock, *Your Brain at Work* (New York: HarperCollins, 2009), 62.
8. Ibid., 6.
9. Ibid., 27.
10. Ibid., 6.

Chapter 5

1. Joyce Barnes, "The Price Tag of Conflict in the Workplace," Mind for Consulting (blog), October 29, 2015, *www.mindforconsulting.com/ uncategorized/the-price-tag-of-conflict-in-the-workplace/.*
2. Dana A. Gionta and Dan Guerra, "How Successful People Set Boundaries at Work," *Inc. Magazine,* April 8, 2015, *www.inc .com/dana-gionta-dan-guerra/how-to-manage-boundaries-at-work.html*
3. David Rock, *Your Brain at Work* (New York: HarperCollins, 2009), 62.
4. Dana Scott and Kathlyn Hendricks, "102: How to Have an Effective Team Without a Leader," *Super Fantastic Leadership Show* (podcast), March 2016, *www.daphne-scott. com/2016/03/102-effective-team-without-leader/*
5. Patrick Lencioni, *Overcoming the Five Dysfunctions of a Team* (San Francisco, CA: Jossey-Bass, 2005), 6.

Chapter 6

1. Larry Bradley, "What Is Chaos?" *Chaos and Fractals* (website), 2010, *www.stsci.edu/~lbradley/seminar/chaos.html.*
2. David Rock, *Your Brain at Work* (New York: HarperCollins, 2009), 122.
3. Ibid., 99.
4. Amy Jen Su, "Signs that You're a Pushover," *Harvard Business Review OnPoint Magazine,* Spring 2017, 27.
5. Beth Howard, "The Secrets of Resilient People," *AARP,* November/ December 2009, 26.
6. Ibid., p. 36.

Chapter 7

1. Kerry Hannon, "How to Love Your Job Again When All You Want to Do Is Quit," *The Practical Guide to Life Hacks,* Spring 2017, 116.
2. Ibid., 117.
3. David Rock, *Your Brain at Work* (New York: HarperCollins, 2009), p. 47.
4. Ibid., 48.
5. Ibid., 223.
6. Ibid., 83.
7. Jennice Vilhauer, "4 Reasons Why Change Is Hard, But Worth It: What to Do When Your Thoughts Get in the Way of Your Goals," *Psychology Today,* June 30, 2016, *www.psychologytoday.com/blog/ living-forward/201606/4-reasons-why-change-is-hard-worth-it.*
8. Stephen Covey, *The 7 Habits of Highly Effective People* (New York: Free Press, 1989), 61.

BIBLIOGRAPHY

Covey, Stephen. *The 7 Habits of Highly Effective People*. New York: Free Press, 1989.

Davis, Josh. *Two Awesome Hours*. New York: HarperCollins, 2015.

Kelly, Matthew. *Resisting Happiness*. North Palm Beach, FL: Beacon Publishing, 2016.

Lencioni, Patrick. *Overcoming the Five Dysfunctions of a Team*. San Francisco, CA: Jossey-Bass, 2005.

Lombardo, Michael, and Robert Eichinger. *FYI: For Your Improvement, A Guide for Development and Coaching*. Minneapolis, MN: Lominger International, 1996–2009.

HBR's 10 Must Reads On Emotional Intelligence. Boston, MA: Harvard Business Review Press, 2015.

Phillips, Patricia Pullam, Jack J. Phillips, and Rebecca Ray. *Measuring the Success of Employee Engagement*. Alexandria, VA: ATD Press, 2016.

Rock, David. *Your Brain At Work: Strategies for Overcoming Distraction, Regaining Focus, and Working Smarter All Day Long*. New York: Harper Collins, 2009.

Sinek, Simon. *Start with Why: How Great Leaders Inspire Everyone to Take Action*. New York: Portfolio, 2009.

INDEX

ABOUT THE AUTHOR

Mary Camuto founded MC Consulting, a firm specializing in leadership and organization development, training design, and group facilitation services in 2002. Her special areas of focus include managing chaos, time, and effective communication. She has spoken at large events about change, leadership, and managing generational differences. She connects energetically with her customers in various forums, such as speaking and teaching, live online training, and face-to-face events with audiences of various generations, levels, and roles.

You can learn more at her website Marycamuto.com.